BIZAR
BERKS

Duncan Mackay is a former winner of the Henry Ford European Conservation Award for Heritage and author of *The Secret Thames* (1992), *Apples, Berkshire, Cider* (1996) and *Eat Wild* (2010). He has contributed to several books and magazines including *England in Particular, Bastions of Berkshire, ECOS, Urban Nature, Great Outdoors, Scottish Hosteller, Cycle* and *Country Living*. He is a former Editor of the Twyford and Ruscombe Local History Society Journal. Duncan is currently Rear Commodore of Henley Sailing Club, his wife Viv is a GP in Berkshire, his son Nick is a marine biologist in Edinburgh and daughter Becky is a photography graduate from University College, Falmouth. Duncan has worked as: Director of the South East region of the Countryside Agency; Technical Director in the Babtie Group; Environmental Manager for Berkshire County Council; and Deputy Secretary of the Commons, Open Spaces and Footpaths Preservation Society. He is currently writing *Long, Slow and Wiggly*, the story of his mainly off-road, folding-bike journey to Cape Wrath from the Isle of Wight.

ALSO PUBLISHED BY TWO RIVERS PRESS

Eat Wild by Duncan Mackay

The Reading Quiz Book by Adam Sowan

Birds, Blocks & Stamps: Post & Go Birds of Britain by Robert Gillmor

Reading Poetry: An Anthology edited by Peter Robinson

Reading: A Horse-Racing Town by Nigel Sutcliffe

Down by the River: The Thames and Kennet in Reading by Gillian Clark

From the Abbey to the Office: A Short Introduction to Reading and its Writers by Dennis Butts

A Much-maligned Town: Opinions of Reading 1126–2008 by Adam Sowan

A Mark of Affection by Adam Sowan

A Ladder for Mr Oscar Wilde by Geoff Sawers

The Stranger in Reading edited by Adam Sowan

The Holy Brook by Adam Sowan

Charms against Jackals edited by Adam Stout and Geoff Sawers

Abattoirs Road to Zinzan Street by Adam Sowan

BIZARRE BERKSHIRE

DUNCAN MACKAY

Illustrated by Sally Castle

TWO RIVERS PRESS

First published in the UK in 2012 by Two Rivers Press
7 Denmark Road, Reading RG1 5PA

www.tworiverspress.com

ISBN 978-1-901677-77-5

British Library Cataloguing in Publication Data. A catalogue record for
this book is available from the British Library.

1 2 3 4 5 6 7 8 9

Two Rivers Press is represented in the UK by Inpress Ltd and distributed
by Central Books.

Cover design, typographic design and illustrations by Sally Castle.

Printed and bound in Great Britain by CPI Antony Rowe, Chippenham
& Eastbourne

To my sister, Ruth Hoare

Acknowledgements

I want to express my many thanks to Sir Michael Parkinson for his generous foreword to *Bizarre Berkshire*. We share South Yorkshire origins where people appreciate self-deprecating humour, albeit much parodied by Monty Python. In many years of watching the legendary 'Parky' in action on TV interviewing politicians and superstars there was always a glimmer of Northern directness and a twinkle of that droll humour. My father still starts letters by writing, 'It's a grim, grey, Northern day' which always makes *me* laugh but it's not everyone's cup of tea. My mother is so gobsmacked that Sir Michael has agreed to this that she has gone to the top of our stairs. Thanks to Professor Ken Olwig from the University of Alnarp in Sweden who is a global academic expert in so many historical, linguistic and cultural aspects of history, landscape and politics on both sides of the Atlantic that it makes my head spin. We share an interest in the origins and the future of local food, cider and commons. Lance Railton at the Ghost Club has prompted my musings on the potential scientific dimension of ghost sightings. Discussion about *Bizarre Berkshire* amongst family members has also produced three previously unrecorded ghostly events.

Thanks to Sally Castle, the inspirational illustrator and designer of the book. Sally's illustrations are conjured from the mists of imagination that most of us cannot even see through let alone shape to beautify the page. Thanks also to the team at Two Rivers Press: the gimlet eye of Adam Sowan and his advice on the nuances of copyright, fair comment and public domain which has allowed more content than I thought possible. Sally Mortimore, Karen Mosman and

Barbara Morris have supported the project from the first twinkle through to full execution. One item that got the chop was my suggestion to sub-title the book 'The X-Flies' as a homage to the TV series *The X-Files*. The joke I was trying to pull off was the tenuous link to the story of the Bucklebury Fly. Clearly the idea didn't fly.

I offer grateful thanks to all the local historians of Berkshire and elsewhere and attendant 'wikinauts', now united by the world wide web. I salute their dedication, diligence and digging abilities. Books like this would not be possible without their research and fascination with the minutiae of past times. I also need to thank Dennis Lowe, for his entertaining descriptions of life on the set of *Alien* working with Ridley Scott and the special effects crew at Bray Studios including my former neighbour Brian Eke from Twyford. As an author and researcher the gift of sight and the ability to type are precious to me. I owe thanks to the staff at Wargrave Surgery, Miss Watson's Royal Berkshire Hospital Eye Clinic and Mr Pailthorpe's team (for easing the Dupuytren's contracture in my hand).

My long nights spent scouring the Internet and reading weird publications have had a profound impact on my family. The children have left home and gone far away and my lovely wife Viv has fallen asleep on the sofa quite a lot. I think I can trace this genetic quirk in the pursuit of bizarre items to my dear father who keeps an attic-full of newspaper clippings of 'interesting things that one day might come in useful'. Sadly, I have used none of them. I am dedicating this book to my sister Ruth who, for reasons of her own, insists that all the handles of the mugs hanging on her kitchen dresser must point in only one direction - at all times. For all those 'out there' just like her, this book is for you too.

CONTENTS

FOREWORD

by Sir Michael Parkinson

Duncan and I share a South Yorkshire inheritance that sees wit and the telling of shaggy dog stories placed high amongst the local measures of social standing. We are both now happily exiled in the green and leafy Royal County of Berkshire that we call 'home' but somewhere deep in our souls our Yorkshire heritage still lurks.

After a career of interviewing people, I'm still fascinated by the art of story-telling. I am always keen to know more about how people create their own place in history. Duncan's little book *Bizarre Berkshire* reveals some outstanding fragments of personal histories as well as moments in Berkshire life that have created national history.

This delightful book is based in the rich seam of doubt and possibility which lies between real events and 'history' as revealed by eye witnesses or recorded by historians. We were not there at the signing of Magna Carta nor at the plundering of the Caversham Shrine so we will never know what really happened, but with the right sort of evidence and our own faculty called commonsense we can begin to draw our own conclusions. This book helps us on that journey of discovery and I hope you will also be amused as you explore the odd corners of the more bizarre parts of Berkshire.

INTRODUCTION
by Duncan Mackay

What makes you interested in something? What catches your attention in a conversation? Is it a hint of mystery or the lure of a secret that might be revealed? Is it a bit of tasty gossip? Perhaps it is the sheer improbability of the topic or the temptation of an impossible situation being true that attracts your intellectual curiosity. We seem to actually *like* the improbable.

Bizarrely, in September 2011, The Guardian reported the apparent discovery that sub-atomic particles called neutrinos could travel *faster* than the speed of light. The discoverers of this phenomenon are hard-core scientific elite, way beyond geek, from the Oscillation Project with Emulsion tRacking Apparatus (OPERA) in Gran Sasso, Italy working with the CERN laboratory in Switzerland. After 3 years of research, firing 15,000 neutrinos 450 miles through the Earth, results showed that the particles arrived 60 billionths of a second faster than light. The theoretical explanations for this are bizarre enough but the truth could be even stranger including the possible existence of other physical dimensions and the potential ability to travel through time. Professor Brian Cox from the University of Manchester said *'If you've got something travelling faster than light... it is a very, very, big deal.'* Sceptical Professor Jim Al-Khalili at the University of Surrey said, *'It's far more likely that there is an error in the data... but if the CERN experiment is correct... I will eat my boxer shorts on live TV.'* Theorists at Dortmund University said it might be due to neutrinos passing through extra dimensions of space-time and *'taking a short cut.'* If the gurus of theoretical quantum physics are talking about short-cuts through space-time then indeed anything might be possible. Keep an open mind, keep watching the skies and watch out for Prof. Jim on TV.

A is for ANKERWYCKE YEW

Hidden away in damp woodland by the northern bank of the river Thames, which cheerily echoes to the shrieking calls of a colony of naturalised wild parakeets, is one of the English-speaking world's most unknown famous trees – the c.2,500-3000-year-old Ankerwycke Yew. It is a tree with a thirty-foot girth that has wisely spread itself and formed a bower of suckers to snuff out all forms of woody competition for its sacred spot. Indeed it has been suggested that a hermit guardian might have once retreated within its hollow centre as an 'ankerage', thus giving the place its unique name. If we still venerated trees as others do around the world, this ancient specimen might be up there with the Buddha's Tree of Enlightenment, or Yggdrasil, the World Tree of the Nordic myths. But we don't pay it much attention at all, although in spring a few visit to see its magnificent display of shiny green and white snowdrops sneaking out through the bare carpet of yew needles and fallen red yew berries. It has the air of being a magical place and lies opposite the 'council-island meadow' or 'meadow of the Runes', the field of mystery and the Anglo-Saxon seat of a witan or council where the results of the consultation with the runes would have been discussed. Runes and yew trees go together; so too, as it might be suggested, do Runnymede, the Ankerwycke Yew and its rune-consulting island.

Here was once a small island or eyot sometimes likened to an eye in the river. In the past the Thames was not the semi-canalised river it is today, plied by pleasure-boats and cruising barges, but a wider, braided stream occupying a substantial, marshy, chalk-girt flood-

Under the shade of the Ankerwycke Yew on 15 June 1215 it is believed that Magna Carta was signed and sealed by King John of England

plain of many shallow channels and islands. On one such island, surrounded by a tangle of braided waters, including the main channel that we know today as the course of the Thames, was the tiny Ankerwycke nunnery. The last remnant lumps of it are now slowly crumbling to dust as the chalky clunch corrodes away. It had been at Ankerwycke since about 1160, and in the thirteenth century was in the ownership of Richard de Montfitchet. Very little is known of its inhabitants or its history until the year 1215. At this peaceful holy place, in the June of that year, trouble arrived in a headlong collision of fate, duplicity and circumstance. Enter John, King of England, and his bodyguard of foreign mercenaries. Here was history: under the shade of the Ankerwycke Yew, on 15 June 1215, it is believed that Magna Carta was signed and sealed.

John was only 'English' when it suited him; he and his brother Richard the Lionheart, were mostly preoccupied with their Angevin properties in France. Just as Richard gave away England to obtain his release from prison so too did John offer up England to the Pope to escape excommunication and get back the 'right' to charge taxes on the wealthy for 'scutage' (to personally avoid having to go to war) and on widow 'relief' (the tax imposed on baronial wives when they remarried). John was forced to focus on England because he eventually lost most of the French lands, which were his main source of finance, as a result of a series of badly managed battles and personal, violent stupidity. In turning the heat on the English baronial class as a new source of revenue he met his match. Magna Carta was therefore less the glamorous statute of liberties for free men that has since been spun but rather an upper class tax revolt. John thought it wise to initiate the proposition so that he would retain the higher authority that his kingly status vainly demanded rather than being forced to submit. However, even as the words were being crafted through several days of negotiations, he was craftily plotting how to get his own back... and certainly had no intention of honouring the charter's words. Within twelve weeks he had persuaded the Pope to completely annul Magna Carta and by autumn was pitched again into battle with the Barons at the siege of Rochester Castle. Appropriately perhaps for such a slippery monarch John died of dysentery in East Anglia. His entrails were buried at Craxton Abbey and his body shipped to Worcester and thus became one of a handful of 'English' kings of Norman descent to be actually buried here rather than France.

Virtually nobody visits the Berkshire island in the Thames where King John probably signed the Great Charter underneath the Yew tree of Ankerwycke

Whilst thousands of gawping tourists visit the Runnymede meadows, the Magna Carta memorial monument erected by the American Bar Association and the area where the assembly of Barons gathered on the Surrey side of the river in 1215, virtually nobody visits the Berkshire 'island in the Thames' where King John probably signed the Great Charter underneath the great Yew tree of Ankerwycke. From a military strategic point of view, hosting the signing ceremony at the Ankerwycke Yew makes absolute sense in case KJ had to make a swift getaway protected by his mercenary bodyguards... it would have been much more effective to dash north knowing that your pursuers would need to mount their horses and find a crossing point over the river to get on your trail.

English literature records the scene in many ways too, with Jerome Klapka Jerome painting perhaps the most fulsome picture as the narrator of *Three Men in a Boat* (to say nothing of the dog). The trio had hitched their camping skiff at Picnic Point, just downstream of the Ankerwycke Yew, and Jerome threads together a golden cloth of imaginary scenes drawn from prevailing Victorian histories, using his great skill as a storyteller. The Ankerwycke Yew was said by Dr Lardener, in his sixteenth-century book *Arboretum Britannicum,* to be about 2000 years old, although he was guessing; it was certainly old in 1215. Henry VIII was believed to have 'wooed' Anne Boleyn under its boughs; a legendary motif of a 'spooning' couple that Jerome K Jerome made much fun of in *Three Men in a Boat* too. It is possible that the tree may have been planted by Celtic tribespeople to mark a place sacred to their belief in water divinities. It is therefore probable that the Ankerwycke Yew marks the former highest upstream point of the tidal Thames. I suggest this because it would have been a significant place to Celtic peoples in thrall to water spirits, and they did plant yew trees to define sacred spots. This conjecture can be compared with the historically recorded traditions of the London Stone a mile or two downstream at Staines. The London Stone or Citty Stone marks the limits of jurisdiction of the City of London as 'keepers' of the *tidal* Thames. Prior to the introduction of hundreds of manmade obstructions such as watermills and weirs the stone marked the upper tidal limit of the Thames. It is dated 1285, and new Aldermen were ceremoniously 'bumped' on it as an initiation rite. In Ankerwycke the sacred nature of the place could have been eventually inherited by the Benedictine nuns after the widespread conversion of the 'heathen' tribal leaders of the Dark Ages by early Christian missionaries. Nobody will ever know the truth of it, and the old yew tree is wisely keeping its own counsel.

B is for BUCKLEBURY FLY

In the crypto-zoological pantheon of bizarre demonic creatures Loch Ness has its Monster, Lambton its Worm, Bodmin Moor its Beast, Surrey its Puma and Bucklebury its... er... fly. The Bucklebury fly, however, is not some rampaging mythical raptor feeding on sheep and virgin sacrifices, but a delightful piece of painted glass above the manor pew of the Winchcombe family in the chancel of Bucklebury church. The fly is believed to have been painted in the seventeenth century, sometime around 1649, and – even more strangely – has its wings on one side of the pane and its body and legs on the other, creating a very lifelike 3D effect.

It is believed by some that the fly has the power of prophecy, and in the past has allegedly predicted, by an unusual form of thought projection – a type of mental telepathy perhaps – that a maid of the parish would one day be Queen. Obviously the odds on this unlikely event becoming true have shortened considerably since November 2010, when the drop-dead-gorgeous Catherine Middleton from Bucklebury became engaged to be married to one Prince William, eldest son of the current heir to the throne, Charles, Prince of Wales. The betting faltered when pictures of her shopping for baby clothes featured in the Daily Mirror on 1 April 2011 (check the date) and collapsed completely when she married him on 29 April in the same year.

The fly was not the only strange thing to have been seen hovering over Bucklebury in recent years; on 3 April 2008 a £15 million RAF Chinook helicopter was seen to touch down for 25 seconds in the Middletons' back garden. An RAF internal inquiry into why a piece of expensive military hardware, one of a type desperately needed by front-line military forces in Afghanistan's Helmand province, was being deployed on joyrides by officers showing off to their girlfriends, was quickly brushed under the carpet. 'Boys will be boys' said an unofficial spokesman by way of explanation... no, they didn't really say that; the MOD said the flight was one of five sorties flown by Wills between 2 and 11 April described as 'contentious'. Prince William learned his flying skills under a secret RAF flying programme code-named 'Project Golden Kestrel', so with such a name the idea of 'fast hovering bird = quick Chinook visit to girlfriend' must have been a perfectly natural consequence. Allegedly, the father of the bride said at the royal wedding reception that he first knew

that his daughter's relationship had become serious when a large helicopter landed in his garden. It beats a spotty youth in a baseball cap driving a Ford Fiesta with a hole in the exhaust tearing up the gravel on the drive. Obviously Mr Middleton might have been misquoted.

Flying Officer Wales's senior officers responsible for his training really got into a spot of bother when someone obtained a Freedom of Information Act request to list the prince's schedule of training flights. These officers were then counselled about their errors of judgement and reminded of their supervisory duties. Dash it, the RAF were even forced to disclose how much it had all totted up to as well. For the record, Prince William's five most contentious trips only cost £86,434. These involved, quite naturally, a trip to see his dad at Highgrove, buzzing his grandma at Sandringham, flying up to a chum's wedding in Hexham, Northumberland, and picking up his brother in Woolwich Barracks to go on a three-day bender of a stag party on the Isle of Wight with his cousin Pete. The *Daily Telegraph* austerely reported that Air Chief Marshall Sir Glen Torpy, the Chief of the Air Staff, had ordered an investigation after details of the flights emerged in the media. But let's get real... give any 23-year-old bloke a massive helicopter, a full tank of petrol, a couple of winks and a nod, and they'd do exactly the same thing. Everybody in the whole world loves Kate and Wills, and all minor tiddly-widdly past misdemeanours have been long forgotten. Just fast-track the babies, dudes...

C is for CARAVANNING

The world-wide modern touring caravan, with its vast array of appliances and creature comforts, and indeed the very philosophy of caravanning for pleasure, was invented in Twyford by a retired Berkshire doctor, William Gordon Stables, in 1885.

The good doctor, who lived at what is now Ruscombe House (then called The Kennels, and formerly the Bowl and Pin pub) from the 1870s to his death in 1910, transformed his garden into a wild space that he called 'the Jungle'. In it he had a shed called 'the Wigwam' in which he wrote over 150 books and articles of a swashbuckling or derring-do nature, sometimes based on his own seafaring experiences across the globe. Gordon Stables was a major contributor to the *Boy's Own Paper,* and one of its original team of writers. Lashings of ginger beer and stashes of cake for adventurous boys were his daily companions long before Enid Blyton reinvented the genre with that wimp of a dog called 'Timmy'. Between 1864, when he married Theresa Williams, and his death, he had six children of his own to amuse. His children's books shaped a generation, and the literary critic Patrick Cosgrave wrote:

> *'There is little, if any, unpleasant snobbery in these stories. Indeed, in the best of them, our young heroes have to bear the extra burden of families fallen on hard times, and this makes the point, in opposition to the snobs they encounter, that what counts is individual worth, loyalty, charity, humanity and courage.'*

Stables was an Aberdeen University-trained medical doctor, and commissioned as an assistant-surgeon in the Royal Navy. In the service he was involved in stopping the African slave trade, but while there he also caught the tropical diseases that led to his medical retirement in 1871. It was possibly this, or his thrill-seeking nature, that led him to the path of drug abuse; he first started experimenting with chloral hydrate in December 1871. 'Chloral', as it was called at the time, is a hypnotic sleep-inducing drug and has been found in modern criminal date-rape cases. It was also recorded in the autopsy results of both Marilyn Monroe and, more recently, Anna Nicole Smith in the USA. Stables was working as a locum doctor at the time, but became so alarmed by his drug-crazed and wayward treatment of his patients that he resigned and took himself off to find a cure for his addiction. He described his condition in June 1872 thus:

> *'My bodily sufferings are very great and my mind is a mere chaos. My face is so thin and white and worn, that I start at my own image in the glass.'*

The contrast with Stables the publicly-acclaimed author of heroic novels for boys and health manuals for girls — he had been called *'the man of hedgerows*

and blowing seas with a big heart for children and a fondness for animals' – could not have been greater. But he did his cold turkey and recovered, although he became estranged from his wife and children, took to whisky, and began fancying the wife of one of his best friends.

But this colourful character had a practical bent: Stables dreamt up the potential for kitting out a large horse-drawn vehicle with everything a sensible person could want for adventures on the road. To this end he created 'The Wanderer', the world's first 'land yacht', pulled by two strong horses called Polly Peablossom and Captain Corn-Flower, and looked after by John the groom. It was equipped with another Polly, a white cockatoo, Hurricane Bob the Newfoundland dog, and Foley the valet – whose critical job was to ride ahead on a tricycle and warn people of the Wanderer's approach. Stables called himself the 'Gentleman Gypsy', derived from his affection for the apparent freedom exercised by real Romany travellers in their cramped horse-drawn homes. The Wanderer, however, was built by the celebrated manufacturers of Pullman coaches in Bristol from the finest mahogany and maple. It was twenty feet long, seven feet wide, and weighed two tons. It was luxuriously furnished with diverse comforts including a bookcase, a china cabinet, a small harmonium, a Rippingilles stove, a piano stool, armchair, mirrors and gilt candle brackets, a guitar, a violin and – last but not least – a navy sword and a good revolver.

It was equipped with Polly the white cockatoo, Hurricane Bob the Newfoundland dog and Foley the valet

In 1885 Dr Stables took off from Twyford for a 1300-mile rambling and tackle-jingling journey to Inverness, and almost single-handedly, apart from the aforementioned bizarre menagerie and hireling chums, created the touring caravan industry. The story of this first-ever tour was celebrated in Stables's book *The Cruise of the Land Yacht Wanderer,* and soon inspired others to follow. In 1907 eleven of the more gregarious caravanning pioneers met to form the Caravan Club of Great Britain and Ireland and elected Gordon Stables as its first Vice-President. In 1909 he was elected President, but clearly was not the clubby sort but more in the mould of a lone ranger of the byways, seeking personal satisfaction in the romance of the road. He never attended any Caravan Club meetings, but died as its first-ever President.

D is for DAY, THOMAS

Wargrave is the last resting place of one Thomas Day, author, who believed in a Rousseau-inspired creed that both people and animals could be improved by moral reasoning. He was a pioneer of the thinking behind what we now call the nuclear family and the 'necessary' subordination of women. Having failed to train a poor orphan girl to be his dutiful wife, he reared a foal that no one else was allowed to touch. Unfortunately, for the second time the theory failed to live up to the test and, on 28 September 1789, the same animal – by now an adult horse – kicked him to death on a bridleway at Bear Grove on Bowsey Hill above Wargrave. Thomas Day was buried at St Mary's Church. Rousseau's theories were controversial even before his own death in 1778 but many live on, such as the notion of a Social Contract, fundamental ideas about inequality, the nuclear family and romantic fiction.

In between birth and death Day had a bizarre life. He was born in June 1748 but left fatherless in July 1749, although his inheritance made him a very wealthy toddler. He had an expensive education and went to Charterhouse School and then to Corpus Christi College, Oxford, when he was 16, although he left without a degree. He hopped the short distance from Oxford to Berkshire and settled in to the family estates at Bear Place near Knowl Hill. A life of idle richness could have been his but for an encounter at Oxford with the influen-

He reared a foal that no one else was allowed to touch

tial Richard Lovell Edgeworth, an Anglo-Irish philosopher and member of the gentry with estates in the bog country of central Ireland. Edgeworth seems to have had the qualities of an unceasing control freak, badgering four wives and fathering twenty children. Amidst all this he still had time to invent the caterpillar track and be a long-term member of a loose intellectual group called the Lunar Society of Birmingham.

When Day met Edgeworth, who had a house at nearby Hare Hatch, he also took a fancy to Edgeworth's sister, but nothing came of the relationship. Day also had a go at romance with both Honora and Elizabeth Sneyd; neither wanted to know, although weirdly they *both* married Edgeworth later (obviously not at the same time... probably). After that Edgeworth and Day cooked up the odd notion that they should use Edgeworth's son Dick as an educational experiment similar to that advocated by Rousseau's book *Emile*. If this experiment had been attempted today, no doubt Social Services would have been alerted at an early stage, but in the eighteenth century it was obviously OK to take Jean-

Jacques Rousseau's theory and turn it into a training programme for children. The project was a failure, but through it Day became an erratic but engaged member of the Lunar Society alongside Edgeworth Snr. This gathering of practical intellectuals met to discuss commercial applications of scientific discoveries and included several Quakers and early industrial chemists. Amongst them were Matthew Boulton, Josiah Wedgwood and Erasmus Darwin, the latter pair being the grandfathers of Charles Darwin. At these meetings Day met Anna Seward, an early romantic poet of the Lichfield set; he also became influenced by the Abolitionist movement agitating for the end of the transatlantic slave trade. Indeed, Day's first literary project was a 1773 poem entitled *The Dying Negro,* co-authored with John Bicknell, which was a great success in influencing public opinion against slavery. In 1776, at the signing of the Declaration of Independence by the US Congress, Day was particularly upset by the Americans' hypocrisy in declaring that 'all men are created equal' yet with signatories owning black slaves on their plantations. Despite this he clearly enjoyed and sympathised with the desire of the American revolutionaries to establish their own republic removed from control of the British Crown.

Edgeworth and Day cooked up the odd notion that they should use Edgeworth's son Dick as an educational experiment similar to that advocated by Rousseau's book Emile

Thomas Day had not neglected his Rousseau creed and visited his hero before his death. His next adventure was to write, in 1783, the hugely popular but instructive anti-slavery children's book *The History of Sandford and Merton,* which described the lives of two boys thrown together and entwined by fateful circumstances. The rich brat being Tommy Merton, and his virtuous but impoverished foil the eponymous Harry Sandford. The principles espoused were that the idle rich were completely useless tossers and that good work was important to everyone, through which heroic virtues could be achieved. This clearly struck a nerve in the newly upwardly mobile strata of eighteenth-century society, where new money derived from new industrial technology and commerce was rubbing shoulders with old money and the county establishment of major landowning estates. The book achieved monstrous sales (for the times), was reprinted three times in a decade, and remained in print for over 100 years. Day added the 1787 book *The History of Little Jack* to his titles, but was already settled into his place in literary history by then.

Perhaps the most bizarre of Day's 'projects' was the rather pervy attempt to train two pre-teenage girls to become dutiful wife material. Clearly if you had the money you could do anything you liked in eighteenth-century England, but hanging around orphanages picking up eleven- and twelve-year-old girls must surely have struck somebody as a bit odd... although apparently not. On this potentially paedophilic adventure he was accompanied by his poetry co-author John Bicknell; they turned up at the Shrewsbury orphanage together to select a 'flaxen-haired beauty' for treatment. They changed her name to Sabrina (after the goddess of the River Severn) Sidney (after Algernon Sidney, a republican theorist executed by Charles II for plotting against him); she was then aged twelve. In London the strange gentlemen popped up at the Foundling Hospital, this time hunting for brunettes, and bagged an eleven-year-old they decided to call Lucretia. Seemingly, nobody in authority batted an eyelid, and the experiment proceeded to an isolated part of Avignon in France for further development in severe treatments to strengthen young minds and bodies. Surprise, surprise but the two girls became quarrelsome, contracted smallpox, nearly died in a boating accident on the river Rhone, and generally proved difficult to train. They all returned to England within eight months. Day decided that Lucretia was 'invincibly stupid' and such an intellectual disappointment that she was pushed off to a local hatmaker and forgotten about. Sabrina survived a bit longer, being subjected to such further tests of stoicism and endurance as having pistols fitted with blanks fired at her (she screamed) and hot sealing wax dripped on her bare arms (she screamed some more). At this point Day gave up and had Sabrina marched off to boarding school in Sutton Coldfield when she was thirteen. Following that, Day settled her in houses in Birmingham and Newport, Shropshire and then, to everyone's surprise, when she was 25 John Bicknell asked Day for her hand in marriage. It was a short affair of just three years before he died, but they produced two sons, one of whom went on to found the (National) Westminster Bank.

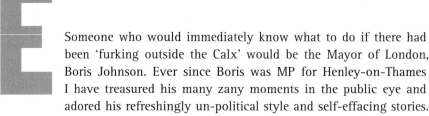

is for **ETON, WALL GAME**

Someone who would immediately know what to do if there had been 'furking outside the Calx' would be the Mayor of London, Boris Johnson. Ever since Boris was MP for Henley-on-Thames I have treasured his many zany moments in the public eye and adored his refreshingly un-political style and self-effacing stories. I particularly relish the non-PC tale that he tells about a cycle ride across London on his old bike when a rather attractive lady cyclist came up alongside him, giving him a winsome smile before calling him a 'Tory twat' and riding off. The fact that Boris finds this funny too is a measure of the man. In his Eton schooldays Boris was also the 'Keeper of the College Wall' and a player in the gloriously bonkers Wall Game. Another player was former Shiplake resident and author of *1984* and *Animal Farm*, Eric Arthur Blair, or 'George Orwell' as the world knows him.

The Wall Game must be one of the most bizarrely eccentric things ever invented, but I sympathise as I too invented a crackers contest when I was at college; albeit at a red brick university in the mid-70s and after a few too many pints of Newcastle Brown Ale. I created 'Le Grand Sel', a game played indoors under fluorescent lighting after the pubs had shut, with a half-filled plastic salt container and a long shiny-topped refectory table. In truth it owed much to Eddie Waring and the ridiculous TV series *Jeux Sans Frontières,* but the rules were simple enough and the object of the two-player game was to tap the salt pot from one end of the table to the other and get it to hang over the end without drop-

The furkers from each team form first, provided the feet do not break the outside line

ping off for 'un point'. I feel certain that the Wall Game probably emerged from some spontaneous nonsense like that but has become institutionalised in the secluded surroundings of Eton, the Galapagos Islands of private education operating under its own peculiar evolutionary rules.

There is something about the Wall Game that recalls the survival of the fittest and the slow pace of evolution too. The last time that *any* team scored a 'goal' in the St Andrew's Day version of the Wall Game was in 1909! Having studied the official rules I'm not surprised, but for the completely uninitiated and the unexposed I will attempt to explain the basics *as I understand them.* I fear that this will be inadequate. The good news is that nobody seems to know even when the game was invented, although the first record of it was in 1766. The rules were first established in 1849, which is five years after the first ever

classic St Andrew's Day match was slugged out in the cold late November weather. These matches are played between the Oppidans and the Collegers, the two types of pupil at the school, with the Oppidans' strength at over 1200 be-suited boys easily outnumbering the opposition selection stock of just 70 King's Scholars. Each team is allowed ten players, with an additional one in reserve in case there is a 'blood injury'. It is a type of football match but played on a pitch that is about 15 feet wide and over 300 feet long adjacent to the famous wall itself, which is slightly bulgy somewhere near the middle but not in bad shape for something built in 1717. There are goals at either end, but not as Geoff Hurst would recognise them, as one is a garden door (and its frame) and the other a tree (below the white line only). A goal, incidentally, is worth a variety of points, with a thrown goal worth nine, a kicked or penalty goal five, and a Shy worth a measly one point. The fact that over 100 successive annual St Andrew's Day matches have ended 0-0 shows that a one-point Shy is not exactly too bad a score. It's not the winning but the taking part. However, I digress. Let's sense some of the occasion before the big St Andrew's Day match by conjuring the Oppidans throwing their caps blindly over the Wall in an impudent challenge to the Collegers before climbing up and over it. The keenest supporters are straddling the Wall atop the brickwork already to get the best bird's-eye views of the tedious progress of the ball below.

Before 1840 the boys were forbidden to go on the river. To get around this 'shirking' was introduced – boys who were rowing covered their faces with a raised arm when stopped by unjolly masters

So, the toss is called and the toss-winning captain makes the decision to play towards the Good or Bad Calx. The first bully of six players each is formed under the ladder, and as always the team that plays towards Good Calx has heads. The umpire rolls the ball in towards the Wall and the game starts with thirty minutes to go before 'Change' (obviously, unless the ball is in Calx when Change is called) and sixty minutes before 'Time'. The team creates a phalanx to protect the ball under the knees or feet of the Second, and the opposition try to force the ball into their control or to create a loose. If the ball crosses the Furrow, then heads will alternate, understandably; this is the same as in all bully-on-the-spot offences. In dead ball situations when it crosses the Furrow and stops or is stopped by players, spectators, inanimate objects or, of course, if the garden wall in Good Calx is touched but outside Furrow, Fly, long, lines and all players performing the role of kicker-out of Calx are naturally behinds. Normally, dangerous play includes kicking, stamping, applying pressure maliciously, kneeing opponents in the head and using clenched fists on their face, but fifteen-yard penalties can be awarded for any play the umpire deems to be outside the spirit of the game, as is also the situation for sneaking or furking. As the game progresses a Calx Bully may be required and the umpire will draw the necessary three lines at right angles to the Wall. The furkers from each team form first, provided the feet do not break the outside line. By now Attacking Wall and Defending Wall will be preparing, provided that inside knees are not prevented from being against the Wall up to the middle line. 'Stop talking' says the umpire, putting the ball on the middle line only. 'Are you ready?' Now it gets really exciting and the tension of the supporters is tangible, waiting to see if there is any Bully reformation appeal required by prior movement before 'Coming' is called. We are getting close to a possible Shy now as Attacking Wall manoeuvres to get the ball off the ground against the Wall with any body parts below the knee, and if a hand touches it behind the Calx line. 'Got it!' is called... got it?

Ironically, Eton College was originally intended (in 1440) for the education of 24 poor and indigent scholars, but is now the World's Most Famous Public School. The College is also well-known for its Field Game, rowing and the Eton Boating Song, but before 1840 the boys were forbidden to go on the river. To get around this 'shirking' was introduced – boys who were rowing covered their faces with a raised arm when stopped by unjolly masters. This meant that they admitted they were being naughty but the masters had to pretend they couldn't see them... sheer inventive brilliance. Eton College's new rowing trench near the Thames Path at Boveney is the 2012 London Olympics rowing venue... obviously a good place to get close to the action – unless there are too many silly furkers on the towpath.

F is for FROXFIELD BRAIN, DOLPHIN AND BUG

During the 1980s and 90s the modern phenomenon known by the name of crop circles began to excite interest throughout the world. These are areas of crops which are found laid flat in patterns, often with a complex inter-layering of stems. The patterns so created before the 1980s were most frequently just simple circles or rings, but these were followed by a massive explosion in creativity and dimension in the designs seen in the crops. The south of England seems to be highly prone to outbreaks of this phenomenon every summer, and much of this occurs across the counties of Berkshire, Hampshire and Wiltshire – in the fancifully named 'Wessex Triangle', although in truth circles have been found everywhere from Cornwall to Scotland.

Farmers are annually both enraged by this spoliation of their crops and intrigued by its additional commercial potential – as people are willing to pay a nominal £1 to walk inside some of the more spectacular formations. The crop circle fraternity, or 'croppies' as they are known, scour the Wiltshire lanes in the summer or fly light aircraft to gain aerial access to remote corners of the Wessex downs. The tourist boards are delighted with the annual influx of visitors as the phenomena have attracted world-wide (or even inter-galactic) foreign tourists and their wallets. The Barge Inn, a community enterprise pub at Honey Street on the Kennet and Avon Canal in the Vale of Pewsey, has become their unofficial summer HQ, and every warm evening will see a crowd discussing the latest sightings, much as twitchers talk up rare birds or train-spotters speak in numbers of exotic bogies. The pub even has its own beer called *Croppie* and a strong cider called *Area 51*.

'Croppies' scour the Wiltshire lanes in the summer or fly light aircraft to gain aerial access to remote corners of the Wessex downs

Causality of these bizarre demonstrations remains a complete mystery, with the claimants to differing theories fighting bitterly amongst themselves to prove their claim as *the* true answer. Principal among the theories is that it is all done by bands of dedicated nocturnal human hoaxers, or alternatively by bands of dedicated nocturnal aliens, or earth energies, or sky-critters, or military satellites. Some theorists have postulated that these alien intelligences are trying to impart

21

messages about the impending return of the ancient gods at the Dawn of the Age of Aquarius to effect a spiritual transformation of humanity, or conversely our impending doom as a species as unseen asteroids (or Planet X or Nibiru) hurtle towards us through the icy darkness of space. The known crop circle hoaxers have declared themselves as a range of 'sceptical' organisations, some of whom have created circles and other formations deliberately to catch out the alien theorists. Foremost amongst these, a few

Rings, circles, dots and a snake-like squiggle appeared at Walbury Hill

years ago, at least in parts of the newsprint media, were two old men from Southampton who allegedly declared that they alone had done every circle in the fields of southern Britain for many years. Unfortunately after they had 'retired' the crop circles continued to form... and indeed proliferate. The BBC's Nicholas Witchell got very excited when he reported live news one morning from the so-called 'Operation Black Crow' using special night vision cameras loaned by the MOD; but it was just a military black op set up to make the leading croppies look foolish. One of the earliest scientific ideas was the 'whirlwind' theory, which then had to evolve into a 'plasma vortex' theory as the circles grew in complexity, and then bow out completely as the circles turned into triangles, squiggles and other bizarre shapes like the 'Mandelbrot' design found at Ickleton near Cambridge.

Some of the more amazing shapes of the time, as the designs exploded in complexity, were those that appeared around the western extremity of Berkshire close to the Wiltshire border. Sometime around 18 August 1991 some *very* weird patterns were pressed into the wheatfields near Froxfield. These included designs such as the 'Froxfield Dolphin', the 'Froxfield Brain' and the 'Froxfield Bug'. The 'brain' was a discontinuous squiggle which someone likened to 'a strand of DNA seen under an electron microscope', although this one covered 800 square metres of land. The 'Froxfield Brain' is so weird that despite the passage of 20 years, and the appearance of thousands of crop circles all over the world from Canada to Indonesia, there has never been another one like it. The 'dolphins' were a series of boat-shaped areas with 'fins', although the one at Froxfield didn't have fins and looked strangely like a pair of weird spectacles, albeit 85 metres long. The 'bug' was a squat sort of 'dolphin' but with four finny things. The debate as to whether these formations are man-made or otherwise is still live, and new theorists should write to the editor of Farmers Weekly immediately.

In recent years Berkshire has received even weirder agri-glyphs, particularly in the west of the county. On 12 June 2010 a very strange complex of rings, circles, dots and a snake-like squiggle appeared at Walbury Hill near Combe. A few weeks later on 30 July two bizarrely near-identical formations appeared on either side of the M4 at Wickham Green. Both had a ring enclosing what looked like a type of abacus with 'beads' on identically spaced sets of sixteen 'strings'. The precision was remarkable and the effort required seems prodigious. The arrangement of beads on the strings caused a ripple of excitement in Turin, because it is just about possible, if you squint long enough from far away, to convince yourself that the image has a passing resemblance to the Turin Shroud. Some writers are now suggesting that the shroud itself was a medieval hoax perpetrated by Leonardo da Vinci, whose image it bears.

Keep watching the fields for signs and portents...

is for GHOSTS: Littlewick Green and Weycock Temple

One of the more peculiar ghost story clusters from Berkshire involves the area around Littlewick Green, Ashley Hill and the former pagan temple at Weycock Hill (not much of a hill, more a low hillock in reality) and although there is a white lady there is also a headless phantom and a Black Dog (or White Dog) tale too. The area of central Berkshire between Twyford and Maidenhead is a flat, fertile plain extensively used for cereal cropping; what used to be a large shallow lake (Stanlake) lay to the south of the area before it was drained by the creation of The Cut in the nineteenth century. In Roman times the same soil fertility (and the probable abundance of game birds) also attracted a fair amount of settlement after the invasion of Britain. This settlement pattern might have been further assisted by the proximity of the 'Camlet Way', the now lost road from St Albans to Silchester, which is believed to have crossed this area.

The Romans worshipped a bewildering range of gods from pagan cults such as Mithraism to Christianity, and after they left a confusing mix of native and imported cults still held sway. Many gods and goddesses, believed to have a controlling influence in a range of domestic and political matters, were invoked whenever necessary at formal temples and in the villas of the settlers. One of the most interesting fourth-century Romano-Celtic pagan temples in Britain was sited at Weycock Hill near Littlewick Green; although nothing remains to be seen on the ground now, there used to be visible chunks of the walls after a crude and destructive excavation of a mound there by landowner Richard Neville in 1847. Its octagonal floor plan can still be seen clearly as an under-soil crop mark (not to be confused with a crop circle!) in dry summers. There are only two other octagonal temples in Britain, at *Venta Silurum* (Caerwent) in south Wales and Pagan's Hill in Somerset. It has been suggested that the temple may have been dedicated to the worship of *Vesta* and hence would have been the home of the Vestal Virgins (*Sacerdos Vestalis*), the only priestesses allowed under Roman law. The virgins, who were recruited as morally and physically unblemished children with still-living parents, were important guardians, six at a time, of the perpetual flame in the temple. *Vesta* was also the goddess of the household hearth around which

They were put to death by being buried alive in underground pits with just three days' worth of food and water

24

so much of Roman life was centred. The virgins spent ten years being trained, ten years as flame guardians and ten years as trainers. If the priestesses allowed the flame to go out, or were unchaste during their 30-year career at the temple, they were put to death by being buried alive in underground pits with just three days' worth of food and water. Under strict Roman Sumptuary (fabric colour) laws the virgins wore three pieces of white clothing: a full length gown (*stola*) decorated with white pearls and a *mamillare* (a band across the chest to accentuate the breasts); a cloak (*palla*) for outside wear, and a head covering for piety (*suffibulum*). In addition, outside the temple they wore white slippers made from the skins of sacrificial animals.

The White Lady used to walk through both walls across the sitting room of Bertha Lamb, who founded the Littlewick Green Women's Institute in 1918

If you do not have the inclination to consider the possibility of ghosts or a dimension of spirits, skip to the next (H) section as we now take a leap of faith to intriguingly attempt to tie in the Weycock temple and its potentially virginal denizens with the local 'White Lady' ghost story. The white ghost has been seen throughout Littlewick Green: at the site of the 'boundary elm'; Green Lane; the Green; Coldharbour; and Knowl Hill. In a house on Green Lane the White Lady used to walk through both walls across the sitting room of Bertha Lamb, who founded the Littlewick Green Women's Institute in 1918. Prompted by this, the Maidenhead Archaeological and Historical Society organised a dig in the 1960s and found human bones, Roman artefacts and the footings of a Roman building in the garden.

Is it possible that these sightings link the lost Camlet Way Roman road and Roman farm track network along which the Weycock vestal virgins might have trod? Is it further possible to wildly speculate that the White Lady is the ghostly apparition of a careless fire-keeper or unchaste virgin put to death in a pit burial? The literature of ghosts indicates a close pairing of sudden or traumatic death and set locations. An archaeological report of a dig in the Weycock Temple area alongside the ex-Great Western Railway line reportedly found some ten-foot-deep and four-foot-wide flint steened (lined) pits described as wells, and a cemetery with human skeletons oriented east-west. There is also a Pitlands Farm in the area.

Feens (Ffiennes) Farm has a legend of a Black Dog, the 'Dog of Feens' as it is called. However, somewhat confusingly there is also a 'White Dog of Feens', the size of an Irish wolfhound, that was allegedly seen by forestry workers around 1985-6 in the woodlands of Ashley Hill, within half a mile of the farm. Interestingly it was said to disappear 'as if running behind a black sheet' on a route from Chalkpit Farm to Feens Farm.

Dorcas Noble is the name of a wronged ghost, a lovelorn young woman, who was betrothed to one of the Nevilles of Billingbear Park. She was murdered in a particularly brutal fashion by having her head hacked off along Green Lane, allegedly by the object of her marital ambitions after he faltered and she resorted to the magical arts to win back his love. Her ghost is headless and mounted on a horse, sometimes with a dog.

All of these ghostly motifs come together at the nearby Seven Stars Inn at Knowl Hill, where not only is there a headless woman but a woman in a white dress escorted by a spectral dog... and just for good measure a man wearing all-black clothes. Finally, there was the ghost of a child in a house at Littlewick, allegedly called Nellie, who so freaked out the occupiers that an exorcism was required.

You must make of these bizarre tales what you will, as there are no forensic reports, no photographic or video evidence, just a rambling dialogue to knit together the fog of time, place and unfortunate circumstance.

H is for HAMMER HOUSE OF HORROR

Bray has been made famous as a village by having dodgy vicars, the one-time World's Best Restaurant at the Fat Duck, and not just one but three Michelin-starred pubs and restaurants. However, to many filmgoers and TV-watching people who lived through the swinging sixties period it was the haunting image of a candle-lit mock-Gothic ruin by the Thames at Bray that got most pulses racing. The mansion that inspired such a response was Oakley Court and its woodland setting next to Down Place, which for a time (1951-1967) was the HQ of UK film production legend Hammer Films. When Oakley Court was left deserted for 14 years after its mildly eccentric owner Ernest Oliver died in 1965, the spooky Gothic architecture was used as a Hammer film backdrop for the last two years of their tenure at Bray. Indeed it was enhanced by shooting many scenes for many schlock-horror films in and around the ivy-clad property at night. Perhaps most famous of these were the Dracula series starring Christopher Lee and Peter Cushing, but other films shot around Oakley Court were The Rocky Horror Show, Half a Sixpence (Tommy Steele), Murder by Death (Peter Sellers) and many of the gore-fest Hammer House films, oozing with newly-visible Technicolor fake blood. The Dracula films were an immediate hit with cinema audiences, and night scenes in the films were lit solely by candles for maximum psychological impact.

The Dracula films were an immediate hit with cinema audiences, and night scenes in the films were lit solely by candles for maximum psychological impact

The list of films included: The Curse of Frankenstein (1957), Dracula (1958), The Hound of the Baskervilles (1958), The Mummy (1959), Captain Clegg (1962), Phantom of the Opera (1962), The Scarlet Blade (1963), Devilship Pirates (1963), Dracula Prince of Darkness (1965), Rasputin the Mad Monk (1965), The Zombies (1966), The Plague of the Zombies (1966), The Reptile (1966), The Mummy's Shroud (1967), and Frankenstein Created Woman (1967); as well as Brides of Dracula and The Curse of the Werewolf. I suspect that you have got the general thematic groove from this selection.

Bray Studios was the stage in the late 1970s for much of the Alien film set modelling when CGI was *not* the norm and sets were laboriously created by hand. Twyford-based special effects technician Brian Eke and Denis Lowe from

Wooburn recall working with legendary film director Ridley Scott on the main Alien spaceship model, when decisions were made on the hoof and woodwork originally destined for one job instantly became exhaust nozzles or similarly inspired modifications. Glue, instinct and adaptability were the key ingredients in film set success back then rather than blue screens, 3D and digital special effects. Authenticity and guile were the other weapons used against the actors to obtain the correct degree of genuine shock... Sigourney Weaver, playing the role of Ripley, is alleged to have said '*All it said in the script was "this thing" emerges...* '

Anyone who has ever seen the film will remember the moment as the alien creature bursts out of John Hurt's stomach and showers the cast in fake blood and real entrails from an abattoir in Slough (as well as blood-soaked oysters and other shellfish squirming in the wound cavity). None of them were told what was going to happen, so it was a genuine shock and at least one actor fainted. Special effects technicians, working with the blood pumps and the framework holding the real John Hurt in place under the fake body, knew that other gory 'terminations' were being planned for other cast members, but even now are reluctant to say what they were. Many people will be happy to leave it that way too. The 'chestburster' alien, as it was labelled in the script, was inspired by a painting from 1944 by Francis Bacon called *Three Studies for Figures at the Base of a Crucifixion*, although the whole series of bizarre creatures were created from drawings by Swiss artist H R Giger. The alien itself was not a robotic model but Bolaji Badejo, a thin 7' 2" Nigerian design student – discovered in a bar – in a latex suit dripping with pints of gooey K-Y Jelly.

It was a genuine shock and at least one cast member fainted

Bray Studios hosted a rare thing during the filming of Alien: a crew who were giving 110% to the making of the film, some grinding out 20-hours days, but also enjoying themselves alongside a driven director. Amidst all the blood, sweat and tears were the lighter moments: Dennis Lowe recalls the studio canteen's 1978 Christmas roast stuffed turkey that reached unbelievable culinary heights... or was it just high? Unknown to the Irish cooks preparing the dinner, one of the security staff used to hide his personal stash of dope in a tin in the kitchen. On discovering this tin of 'herbs' they added the entire contents to the sage and onion stuffing mix. At this point the canteen was graced by a couple of passing River Police officers who neatly parked their shiny launch alongside the Thames-side lawn and, feeling peckish, joined in the festive feast. 'These stuffing balls are very tasty' said one. Three hours later, two very stoned officers had to be escorted from the premises and taken to Windsor in a squad car...

that had been surreptitiously rigged by giggly and giddy film crew members with impromptu 'special effects' such as small detonators under the bonnet and nuts and bolts in the hub caps.

Oakley Court is now a fabulous hotel with lawns leading down to the river Thames and superb facilities, albeit with as much 'atmosphere' as your imagination can conjure. Before it became a hotel the house had a handful of owners in its relatively short history. The original house was built as a French chateau-style wedding present for Sir Richard Hall-Saye's young bride Ellen Evans in 1859 following their marriage in 1857; it passed through several owners before becoming the *unofficial* HQ of the French Resistance during the Second World War, when it was owned by a French diplomat who entertained well and probably had a decent cellar. It is rumoured that General de Gaulle visited sometimes and stayed in one of the rooms, although probably sleeping diagonally across a bed as he was very tall even without his kepi hat.

is for IRISH-DUTCH WAR OF 1688

In the battle between the competing forms of Christianity in Britain the faith of the monarch has always been important. 1688 was a major pivotal point in the struggle for supremacy between Catholicism and Protestantism because of the reign of James II, which had begun in 1685. James was avowedly Catholic and sought to re-establish the Church of Rome by policies of enforcement which were applied rigorously after his enthronement. This was resented strongly, and secret messages were sent to his Protestant son-in-law in Holland, William of Orange, urging him to raise an army to invade the country and restore the Church of England. Alarmed by the potential invasion of his shores, and the clear threat to his faith, the king sent for Catholic Irish troops to supplement his own army of 24,000, but the tactic backfired because of disaffection by the English soldiery. Nevertheless, when on 5 November 1688 William of Orange landed, unopposed, at Brixham on Torbay, Devon with 12,000 Dutch troops to start what became known as the 'Glorious Revolution', James was still ready to protect his throne and assembled his much larger army on Hounslow Heath.

At this point all the action, indeed the only serious action, switched to Berkshire. William's troops advanced to Hungerford in the west of the county. James sent a force of Irish dragoons around mid-November to hold Reading and to dig in on the low bluffs above the river Loddon at Twyford against the invaders. The townspeople of Reading were much alarmed by the large force of Irish troops and believed a rumour that they were going to be massacred when they were at church on the Sunday. Other rumours were circulating of massacres, lootings and burnings in the surrounding villages, and a group of townspeople decided to send an urgent emissary to Hungerford to alert the Dutch to the situation in Reading. The secret runner was John Westmorland, a humble clothier, who legged it through the out-posted Irish troops to the Bear Hotel in Hungerford. William heard the appeal for assistance and decided to act. On 9 December he instructed the Count of Nassau to take 650 troops, mainly assembled from crack cavalry units and foot soldiers, to save the people of Reading.

For a short time Reading Market Place was filled with the fierce sounds of battle and the shouts of the wounded

Anticipating that the Irish forces would have the main roads from the west and south well manned with defenders, the Dutch cavalry decided to go north and sneak into Reading using the little lane from Pangbourne. As a plan it worked

sufficiently well to gain the slight advantage of surprise, and the main force aimed directly for the temporarily garrisoned troops in the centre. For a short time Reading Market Place was filled with the fierce sounds of battle and the shouts of the wounded. At the critical moment in the hand-to-hand skirmishing the Dutch regrouped and mounted a full cavalry charge at the Irish troops. At this the Irish chose to retreat with 20 dead bodies of their comrades lying in the square, leaving behind 40 wounded as prisoners of the townspeople. In full flight towards Twyford, the 300 remaining troops of James II were followed by 50 of the Dutch contingent to the marshy land near where two fords cross the river Loddon near its confluence with the Thames. Contemporary reports of the action here reveal that at one point a single Dutch cavalryman was seen riding his horse into the Loddon in pursuit of 12 Irish soldiers. On the bluffs above, looking down on the river, were encamped three regiments of horse from King James's army led by Sir John Lanier and Sir John Fenwick. Nobody moved to help the Irish in the water, and thereafter the natural boundary of the war was set at Twyford... though the Dutch returned to Hungerford, and the (by then leaderless) English regiments approached William to join his cause and were sent to defend Reading. James despatched Commissioners to treat with William at the Bear Hotel in Hungerford in early December and terms were discussed, but inconclusively. A few weeks later, around the winter solstice, James fled to France, dropping as he did so the Great Seal of England in the Thames at Horseferry Steps in Westminster.

Thus Berkshire witnessed the only bloodshed of the 'Glorious' or otherwise so-called 'Bloodless' Revolution of 1688.

J is for JETHRO TULL

To all followers of 1970s rock and roll bands the name Jethro Tull conjures up the image of wild-haired lead singer Ian Anderson and his maniacal flute-playing. To students of agricultural history, and indeed anyone interested in the social history of the Agricultural Revolution in England, the name, like that of 'Turnip Townsend', is a direct link to a period of agrarian innovation and change. This was a slow but spasmodic series of upheavals which contributed to the downfall of the English peasant class and promoted the types of agricultural techniques which have partially created the palimpsest of landscapes visible in modern Britain today.

Jethro Tull was born at Lower Basildon, in the narrow valley of the Thames between Pangbourne and Goring, in 1674. Although his family were gentrified landowners, and he might have expected to manage the estates, Jethro went up to St John's College Oxford when he was 17 and went on to Gray's Inn to be trained as a barrister. It is not clear if he ever sat a degree or seriously took up the law as an occupation, but he was admitted to the Bar in May 1699. Following this success he toured Europe looking into agricultural practices before returning to his father's new farm later in 1699, and married Susannah Smith from Burton Dassett. He farmed for ten years at Howberry Farm near Wallingford,

A Method of Introducing a sort of Vineyard Culture into the Cornfields in order to increase their Product and diminish the Common Expense

now in Oxfordshire. However, ill health affecting his lungs forced him to travel to France and Italy in search of a 'cure', as was the fashion in the eighteenth century for those wealthy enough. There he became a close observer of the agricultural techniques of the French and Italian vineyard owners who hoed the weeds from the ground between their vines by hand or with small plough-like hoes pulled by horses rather than the heavier plodding oxen almost universally favoured for ploughing in England at the time. Tull was amazed by this bizarre performance and incredulous that they did not have to manure between the crops nor let the land periodically lie fallow so as to restore its fertility. When he returned to Britain in 1714 and inherited his new farm near Hungerford called 'Prosperous' from a dodgy uncle, he was determined to see if he could apply the same techniques. Tull did so for thirteen consecutive years, which was as revolutionary a practice as was possible to conceive for the time. The horse-hoe copied from the French vineyards of Languedoc became the

literary star of Jethro Tull's world-famous 1733 pamphlet whose grand title befitted its revolutionary zeal:

> 'The Horse-Hoeing Husbandry or An Essay on the Principles of Tillage and Vegetation wherein is shown a Method of Introducing a sort of Vineyard Culture into the Cornfields in order to increase their Product and diminish the Common Expense'.

All major agricultural changes were seen, quite understandably, as a threat to the peasant way of life, and resistance to such innovations was fierce; it is most likely that the adaptation of his inventions for practical use in the fields suffered from criminal sabotage at the hands of his workers. It is hard to conceive now, with fields devoid of people, just how many folk were once employed there labouring through all seasons and in all weathers in a constant quest for local sustenance and landowner profit.

Tull's other big idea was the seed drill, dating from 1701; allegedly it came to him while watching the operation of organ pipes in his local church, opening and closing to create a note. This revolutionary tool could operate like an organ with holes opening in a series of pipes linked to a hopper box of seeds. This planted the seed in uniform, equally-spaced rows, using a much smaller amount of seed in easier-to-reap rows than the more blanket and potentially wasteful way of broadcasting the seed by hand-thrown methods. This innovation was strongly opposed even by his own labourers, who were called upon to try out various modifications to the drill on the Tull landholdings but who saw it as a means of unnaturally speeding up the seasons of the agricultural calendar and, more pertinently, reducing the numbers of seed-sowers. As a consequence, it wasn't until the nineteenth century that Tull's labour-saving ideas were put into widespread practice, as more and more people were forced off the land through ever-increasingly impactful enclosures of commons and were obliged to seek industrial employment in the developing towns.

It is bizarre to think that but for inventors like Tull the fields might still be full of people and crops grown in haphazard patterns, rather than in straight tramlines managed by ever more elaborate and expensive machines but dramatically few operators. Tull's historical epitaph therefore is that he is now regarded by the modern mechanical farming elite as the Father of British Agriculture.

K is for **KNIGHTS TEMPLAR**

It's now almost fashionable to be a Knights Templar scholar, with so many books and films squirting out vast oceans of claims and counter-claims about who they were and what they did. Much of this has been captured in the High Court lawsuit proceedings brought against the author of *The Da Vinci Code* by the authors of *The Holy Blood and the Holy Grail* which ended rather ignominiously. Whether you want to believe in the secret of Jesus's bloodline being carried mysteriously through a line of Merovingian kings in France, or clues to enormous Holy Grail secrets to be found under the flagstones of St Sulpice church in Paris, is entirely up to you. Clearly the nine knights who founded the order in 1118 after the capture of Jerusalem on 15 July 1099 during the First Crusade were not going to be able to physically protect all the pilgrims on all their long straggling routes from Europe to the Middle East. They were in Jerusalem to dig beneath the al-Aqsa mosque where the original Temple of Solomon on the Temple Mount was located. Theories aplenty abound as to what they were seeking, including the legendary or real Ark of the Covenant, but for several years they excavated beneath the Mount, whose huge Cyclopean walls can still be seen; the last remaining visible element of it being the so-called 'Wailing Wall'. What was found there is even now not known, but it is certain that for nine years after 1118 there were still only nine knights, and the pilgrims were left to fend for themselves. It wasn't until 1127 that Bernard of Clairvaux, a member of the Cistercian Order, set about popularising the 'Poor Fellow-Soldiers of Christ and the Temple of Solomon', later 'Knights of the Temple' and then shortened further to 'Knights Templar'. It is from this point that the donations of land and money poured in from the wealthy European nobility, and the Order prospered.

They became extraordinarily powerful and, in some places, built their curiously round temples

The Knights lived under a vow of individual poverty, but with so much wealth held by the Order itself, which was not bound to a rule of poverty, they had little need to worry about where the next handout was to come from. They became extraordinarily powerful and, in some places, built their curiously round temples. If you see the word 'temple' on an Ordnance Survey map it might be associated with a Templar landholding or building. Temple tube station in London reflects this, as does Bristol Temple Meads station. In Berkshire, the hamlet of Temple by the Thames near Bisham is a reminder of their once mighty power, as is Templeton between Kintbury

and Inkpen. The wildlife trust nature reserve near Inkpen called the Crocus Field is believed to be a remnant of the Templars' travels to the Middle East, where the dried stamens of irrigated fields of crocus plants make the highly treasured and colourful spice saffron, which is currently worth about £4000 per kilo. Whether the origin of the croci in Kintbury is wholly true is not exactly established as historical fact through documentation, but it makes a terrific story. The origin of the crocus fields that gave Saffron Walden in Essex its name is well attested.

One of the more bizarre aspects of the Knights Templar that we still respond to is the echo of the massacres and round-up of 13 October 1307, which is strongly believed to be the origin of the unlucky nature of Friday the 13th. In truth it is the usual story of greed and corruption, but this event was stimulated by a conspiracy between a Pope and a King of France. That such a widespread attack was conducted mainly in secret, given the communications of the age,

The massacres and round-up of 13 October 1307 is strongly believed to be the origin of the unlucky nature of Friday the 13th

is remarkable enough, although its impacts were mainly felt in France and Italy. Pope Clement V wanted to reduce the power of the Templar Order, and Philip IV of France wanted their property. In an age where the charge of heresy carried the penalty of death preceded by torture and confession 'to purify the soul', the condemnation of the whole Order by Pope Clement resonated throughout the Holy Roman Empire. The English authorities were less vigorous; some Templar wealth simply 'migrated' to their companion order the Knights Hospitaller, and the knights themselves were spared the massacres of France. In Scotland the Templars may have found a sanctuary of sorts from persecution and confiscation, and it is alleged by some that a Knights Templar fleet of ships escaped from France and took haven in Scottish ports. It was ostensibly all over for the Knights Templar when the shifty Pope formally dissolved the Order in 1312.

In Berkshire the name Temple derived from Knights Templar landholdings which can still be found lurking at Bisham, Brimpton and Templeton. In addition the Knights Hospitaller held land at Greenham, a preceptory was founded there around 1180 on land given by the Countess of Clare and Gervase Paynell. After the last preceptor died in 1442 it was absorbed, in 1445, on the direction of the Grand Master of Rhodes, to be part of the estates held by the Prior of England. It was all grabbed by Henry VIII during the Dissolution of the Monasteries in 1540.

The Bisham Preceptory was founded in or after 1139 by Robert de Ferrers but dissolved during the events of 1308-12, and later part of the site was used by the Augustinian Order for its own priory. What is left of the Templar Preceptory has been absorbed into the building now called Bisham Abbey, owned by the Sports Council Trust Company. The Brimpton Preceptory was founded on a grant of land from Simon de Ovile in 1198 and was taken over by the Knights Hospitaller but dissolved by 1276; by 1338 it had become part of the Greenham operation. The Templeton Camera seems to have been a small hostel or hospice originally but was apparently absorbed into private ownership at an early date – possibly even before Friday 13 October 1307.

L is for LAMBOURN VALLEY RAILWAY

During the years of Railway Mania, as it became known, there were so many Private Acts of Parliament being promoted to create new railways that the entire business of the state nearly gummed up completely. Once the powerful companies like the Great Western (GWR) really got into their commercial stride they were either building branch lines to all parts of the countryside or acquiring the small rural-serving companies like voracious predators. Soon very few areas of populated Britain were not served by their own branch line. Many of these were launched with great flourishes of civic pride, lengthy speeches, church hall bunting and free country beer. However, some parts of the country were bypassed completely by this new technology; amongst them was the Lambourn Valley in the Berkshire Downs, which resisted the railway mania for over six decades following the opening of the Stockton and Darlington Railway in 1825.

The peace of the Berkshire Downs was not to remain so for ever and in 1897 up stepped Colonel Archer Houblon of the Welford Park Estate to the footplate, so to speak, and summoned into steamy life the Lambourn Valley Railway Co. (LVR). This was Railway Mania on a shoestring, with virtually no major sources of capital and only vague anticipation of making a healthy profit at some point in the future. The line was officially opened on 2 April 1898 and ran the 12 miles to Newbury in 40 minutes or so, depending upon time spent to stop at passenger-controlled halts. There were (eventually) 11 official stations: Newbury, Newbury West Fields Halt, Speen Halt, Stockcross and Bagnor Halt, Boxford, Welford Park, Great Shefford, East Garston, Eastbury Halt, Bockhampton Crossing, and Lambourn.

This was Railway Mania on a shoestring, with virtually no major sources of capital and only vague anticipation of making a healthy profit at some point in the future

Work was completed by the contractors over the winter of 1897-98 with the trackbed and lines laid using their own loco *Ernest*. This engine was also used for running trains from one end to the other for Directors' inspections, but without passengers or freight. The all-important inspection by the Board of Trade took place on 31 March 1898 and the operating licence was issued very shortly afterwards. There were two stipulations made on the line by Col. Yorke, the

Government Inspector: traffic could not exceed 25 miles per hour, and axle loadings could not exceed 8 tons. However, there were one or two problems still to resolve before the first train proudly used the line... er... there was no train. With no money left after construction, the LVR Co had to rent a loco (an old tank engine, No 1384) from the much larger GWR in order to even start to pick up fare-paying passengers. The LVR Chairman, Colonel Houblon, also had to stump up the cash to buy four old ex-GWR carriages costing a total of £1300. He insisted that each one had a plate attached to it stating that it was the property of Colonel Archer Houblon, just in case they went missing in the night! Although the *official* public opening day of 4 April 1898 was eagerly anticipated by local people, the private launch took place with much ado and celebrations on 2 April. No. 1384 was gaily strewn with foliage, union jacks were fixed in sockets, and even a picture of Queen Victoria was put in pride of place above the buffers in front of the smoke-box. The guard at Newbury station asked guests to take their seats in the four resplendent (if antique) carriages at 11.00 prompt, and around ten minutes later the official inaugural trip of the Lambourn Valley Railway commenced, with Mr G Mount, MP for South Berkshire, and the company's General Manager, Mr Gipps, riding the footplate all the way to Lambourn. In the first week of public service over 900 people used the five daily services, and in the first few months extra wagons had to be hired to transport horses from the famous Lambourn racing stables to courses all over the country. Hoorah for rural railways! As Sir John Betjeman once opined, his perfect job would have been to be a stationmaster on a small rural branch line railway. The LVR might have been the ideal place.

After chuffing up and down the Lambourn Valley in splendid style the beautifully liveried locos and carriages made it to the turn of the new century

With no locos of its own, and the GWR not wanting to lease 1384 to a rival operation longer than it had to, Houblon once again dipped into his deep country gentleman's pockets to purchase two new jaunty side tank engines. These were bought from a Gateshead company for £2660 with the aim of starting work with them in October 1898. The engines were called by the delightfully olde worlde Kingdom of Wessex names *Aelfred* and *Ealhswith*, followed in 1903 by another called *Eadweade*.

The good news about the first year of operation was that the railway made around £1000 in profit... however, this did not include the money owed to Col. Houblon. After chuffing up and down the Lambourn Valley in splendid style the beautifully liveried locos and carriages made it to the turn of the new century, but they were beginning to get a bit rough in the chuff. However, by 1904 the predatory GWR came sniffing around with an offer to buy the branch line for £50,000; the offer was rejected, but the GWR suggested that it lease its new steam railcars to the LVR for an attractive £420 a year. At this point, no doubt, Col. Houblon saw the possibility of getting his cash back, and sent the lovely liveried locos and all the rolling stock off to Swindon to be flogged to the highest bidder. It was the beginning of the end for the quixotically independent LVR.

The new rail service, using single unit steam railcars, worked fine for a while, but by 1905 there was a simple but bizarrely unique Lambourn Valley problem. The small steam boilers on the railcars had become furred up with lime-scale after a diet of local chalk-stream water for their inner workings. As these asthmatic railcars wheezed along the track the long-suffering paying passengers made their feelings known; even in an era when life was comfortably slow they still wanted to reach their destinations. On 19 July 1905 it was all over, and a final meeting of the Boards of the GWR and LVR took place at Paddington station to seal the deal. RIP, LVR.

M is for MONTEM MOUND

A curious little grassy knoll, not far from the A4 and sitting somewhat uncomfortably in front of the Slough Ice Rink, has a spectacularly interesting history. This is the Montem (meaning 'mountain') or the Salt Hill, and may be the last faded remnant of a rarely surviving form of gathering to propitiate the pre-Christian Celtic gods and goddesses. There are a few remaining Harvest Hills which purported to serve a similar purpose and relied possibly on processional forms of worship which wound round the slopes of the mound like a coil to the summit. In the case of the Salt Hill rituals the journey from the past to the present is much more uncertain. There is a theory that Henry VI, when setting up Eton College, wanted to celebrate a connection between himself and the legendary Celtic Kings of yore. He therefore (allegedly) insisted that the college observe certain customs related to the Celtic quarter-year calendar events: Samhain (c 31 October), Imbolc (c 31 January), Beltain (c 1 May) and Lughnasadh (c 1 August). The Salt Hill events that follow were originally held in January corresponding with Imbolc before being moved in 1758 to Whitsun in May, when it was warmer. There was also an Eton custom, derived from the Abbey of Bec in Normandy, which involved the boys catching a ram loosed into the fields after harvest; but this was discontinued when the 'catching' apparently degenerated into the reduction of a hobbled ram to pulp with clubs.

Montem Mound, therefore, is not quite clearly identifiable as a corrupted harvest hill; indeed it is usually identified most closely with a Norman motte, but it does have a long history of the salt ceremony relating back to an Eton College Book of Customs from 1561. At this point it is recorded that the boys were sprinkled with salt as a form of initiation, but the event was held at the mound and not at the school itself, two miles away. Salting boys in that way might also mean to imbue them with wit. Perhaps too much wit was imparted, because by 1799 it had become a circus to pay for the school captain's Cambridge University fees (just don't tell the Secretary of State for Education about this wheeze). Now it involved royalty, royal hangers-on and crowds of locals. The event happened once every three years, and this account from the Slough Courier in May 1799 describes the witty, if windy, scene:

It does have a long history of the salt ceremony relating back to an Eton College Book of Customs from 1561

'Yesterday this triennial ceremony took place, with which the public are too well acquainted to require a particular description. A collection, called Salt, is taken from the public, which forms a purse, to support the Captain of the School in his studies at Cambridge. This collection is made by the Scholars, dressed in fancy dresses, all round the country. At eleven o'clock, the youths being assembled in their habiliments at the College, the Royal Family set off from the Castle to see them, and, after walking round the Courtyard, they proceeded to Salt Hill in the following order: His Majesty, his Royal Highness the Prince of Wales, and the Earl of Uxbridge, Their Royal Highnesses the Dukes of Kent and Cumberland, Earl Morton, and General Gwynne, all on horseback, dressed in the Windsor uniform, except the Prince of Wales, who wore a suit of dark blue, and a brown surtout over. Then followed the Scholars, preceded by the Marechal Serjeant, the Musicians of the Staffordshire Band, and Mr. Ford, Captain of the Seminary, the Serjeant Major, Serjeants, Colonels, Corporals, Musicians, Ensign, Lieutenant, Steward, Salt Bearers, Polemen, and Runners. The King and Royal Family were stopped on Eton Bridge by Messrs. Young and Mansfield, the Salt Bearers, to whom their Majesties delivered their customary donation of fifty guineas each.

At Salt Hill, his Majesty, with his usual affability, took upon himself to arrange the procession round the Royal carriages; and even when the horses were taken off, with the assistance of the Duke of Kent, fastened the traces round the pole of the coaches, to prevent any inconvenience. After the young gentlemen walked round the carriage, Ensign Vince and the Salt Bearers proceeded to the summit of the hill; but the wind being boisterous, he could not exhibit his dexterity in displaying his flag, and the space being too small before the carriages, from the concourse of spectators, the King kindly acquiesced in not having it displayed under such inconvenience. The Scholars partook of an elegant dinner at the 'Windmill Inn,' and in the evening walked on Windsor Terrace. The profit arising from the Salt collected, according to account, amounted to 800 pounds.'

The boys' dresses and hats for the 1799 procession were all made by Mrs Snow, a Windsor milliner, and the sum collected was 'less costs of damage and expenses'. At this time real salt was exchanged for money from travellers passing on the roads in the surrounding area and little blue tickets were issued in receipt of monies, upon which were written Latin mottos such as *Mos Pro Lege* (Custom before Law) or *Pro More et Monte* (On behalf of Custom and the Mound). There was even a racket in punning poetry of the worst and most incestuous Eton doggerel kind; it was shouted to the crowds and sold as souvenir copies from the back of carts; amongst the greatest characters in this trade was one poor benighted Herbert Stockhore from a bricklaying family in Windsor who obviously had, as we would now call it, 'mental health issues'.

Whether or not Herbert knew that he was making a complete arse of himself, or whether he cared, is open to conjecture, but he was *the* Montem Poet from 1784 to 1835, so he was probably getting paid. Playing the dupe in this manner also involved wearing patchwork leggings, an old military uniform, and a conical hat with a tasselled fringe whilst riding round the crowds on a donkey cart spouting clever nonsense verse, frequently written in Latin by the smart little tykes who penned it back in college. I'm sure Lord Sugar's TV apprentices should be set this challenge, with or without an MBA in doggerel verse salesmanship.

Playing the dupe in this manner also involved wearing patchwork leggings, an old military uniform, and a conical hat

In the nineteenth century the Salt Ceremony became a massively popular event, especially after the coming of the railways, and the cheap excursion trains from London used to bring thousands to Slough to be part of the merry throng – or huge drunken mob with 'immoral tendencies', depending upon where you were stood. Naturally these occasions attracted both eccentric and criminal behaviour, and rioting was an ever-present concern. The arrival en masse of the lower orders at the events in 1841 and 1844, with the much-reduced collection bag for the Senior Scholar (down from £1000 to just £200) from the impecunious merry-makers, caused a re-think at Eton. The Headmaster and Provost simply banned it *for ever*. As a result Questions were asked in the Houses of Parliament by an Old Etonian MP about reversing the decision and changing the law so that demanding money in the streets in this way would not be regarded as either Vagrancy or Highway Robbery. The Home Secretary replied that Her Majesty Queen Victoria had been informed of the decision and been advised that the school was perfectly competent in reaching its own decisions in the matter... and that was that.

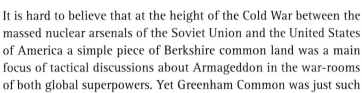

N is for NUCLEAR COWS

It is hard to believe that at the height of the Cold War between the massed nuclear arsenals of the Soviet Union and the United States of America a simple piece of Berkshire common land was a main focus of tactical discussions about Armageddon in the war-rooms of both global superpowers. Yet Greenham Common was just such a subject, and would have been one of the primary targets for the first wave of Soviet ballistic missiles should an attack have been ordered against the Western Powers. However, it is difficult to conceive of a more bizarre scenario than the fact that the *whole* of the Greenham Common cruise missile launch centre, including the hardened silos, the runways and the entire air base bristling with the highest forms of legally authorised 'shoot-to-kill' military forces, was subject to legally registered rights of common to graze cows and to dig gravel. It is entirely unlikely that Mikhail Gorbachev would have said 'Stop the SS-20 missile launches – there are reports of commoners' cows near the silos!'.

It is, however, true that the whole airbase was registered under the Commons Registration Act of 1965 as common land; commoners' rights were confirmed over the same area for both Crookham and Greenham as they lay contiguous to one another, and rights over one stretched to rights over the other. Naturally, given the possibility that the American military forces guarding the cruise missiles might use deadly force against both commoners and their cows if they had got through the perimeter fences, there wasn't a great scramble to exercise the rights of common during the period of renewed USAF occupation between 1980 and 1992, although some attempts were made. Rights of common and common land are cultural treasures which pre-date the Norman Conquest and owe their origins to the communal control of shared natural resources. As the population of Britain grew, the use of common rights was further refined as one of the principal features of the manorial system of land tenure. Common rights are therefore one of our great articles of cultural and legal heritage, older than our magnificent medieval cathedrals in many cases. But formerly they were treated with general political indifference and a cavalier disregard to their continuing preservation; it would be difficult to imagine the cloisters of Salisbury Cathedral being used as a cruise missile launch pad.

Stop the SS-20 missile launches – there are reports of commoners' cows near the silos!

At Greenham and Crookham the commoners exercised their rights until 1941, when the War Department invoked its temporary Second

World War emergency powers to establish an airbase. It should have given the land back at the cessation of hostilities, but there was always another war to justify not doing so: firstly the Berlin Blockade, then the Korean War, followed by the Cold War. After France kicked US forces out of its backyard in the late 1960s the British government decided to offer to host the displaced military machinery in the UK, and in 1977 the USAF thought that Greenham Common's long runway would be just perfect for its massive KC-135 tanker aircraft to use. After enormous public opposition the plan was forced out, to general local relief; but something even deadlier was lurking in the woods. The SS-20 Soviet mobile missile launcher was being developed for dispersal into the vast taiga woodlands of Siberian Russia, whence it could ping deadly warheads with great accuracy and be virtually undetectable. Enter the BGM-109G Gryphon Ground Launched Cruise Missile (GLCM) into the fray,

The Women's Peace Camp was established outside the base entrance and, with the other eventual 39 camps around the perimeter fence, remained there for 19 years

and hello Greenham Common back in the merde. The USA wanted to base 464 GLCMs in Europe with Greenham's share being set at 100 missiles. The Campaign for Nuclear Disarmament said 'oi!' and battle was joined. The military plan was potty from the outset; as soon as the spy satellite's alarm signal showed that the Soviets had launched their missiles, the GLCMs at Greenham would rush out onto the pot-holed local roads or the traffic-congested M4 or A34 and poodle off to pre-determined locations and launch their missiles in retaliation, in the forlorn hope that they wouldn't meet a broken-down bin lorry in Newbury en route. As an alternative, the GLCMs would trundle around Berkshire's byways in a random but continuous dispersal only to invite a veritable shower of air burst Soviet nukes to reduce Berkshire, Hampshire, Wiltshire and Oxfordshire to a smoking, lethally radioactive hole, denuded of all life for the next 40,000 years. To facilitate this madness the military built six hardened shelters to house the missiles and launchers. These monstrous constructions had reinforced concrete ceilings covered in a nine-foot-thick layer of sand, then a vastly expensive titanium plate, followed by another six feet of concrete and topped by a thick layer of clay. Each shelter had nuclear blast-proof hydraulic doors – and enough flame-grilled cheeseburgers to last to the end of the world, or three days, whichever the longer.

In 1981, when the plan to build the missile silos became public, the Women's Peace Camp was established outside the base entrance and, with the other eventual 39 camps around the perimeter fence, remained there for 19 years in continuous opposition to the military presence. There were many attacks on the fence and sporadic invasions of the dangerous military landscape. The fence was six miles in length, but in December 1982, a year ahead of the arrival of the missiles on giant C-5A transport planes, 30,000 women joined hands to encircle it in protest and captured the media headlines for years to come. There was little sign of a reduction in US-Soviet aggression until a bizarre meeting between Mikhail Gorbachev and Ronald Reagan in Reykjavik in 1986, when both leaders chose to ignore their hawkish military briefs and start the process to remove all the deadly GLCMs from Europe. The beginning of the end for Greenham Common's cruise missile launchers began at that point, and by a seeming miracle the warheads had disappeared by March 1991, and the entire base was declared surplus to requirements and put up for sale in February 1993. This was not the last riposte for the commoners, however, as MOD lawyers had completed the controversial legal process to remove their rights of common in 1991, ahead of the proposed sale. Amid much local indignation and some incredulity the lawyers had proceeded, however... to make some very basic legal mistakes. Although they were aware of the Greenham commoners' rights they failed to realise that the Crookham commoners also had rights over Greenham, and that de-registering one group of pesky commoners would not alter the protected status of the common one jot. Newbury District Council (now West Berkshire Council) had the breadth of vision to acquire Greenham Common from the MOD and to embark on a major environmental programme to restore the vast majority of the airbase to its pre-military occupation heathland condition and to reinstate commoners' rights. Now commoners' cows quietly graze the common once more; so, in football score terms, cute cud-chewing cows 1, mad nuclear armed military despots 0.

O is for **OUR LADY OF CAVERSHAM**

Somewhere in Caversham, probably close to St. Peter's Church and St. Anne's Well, possibly on the area now occupied by the pleasant ruins of Caversham Court, was one of the most important centres of medieval pilgrimage in Europe. It is hard to believe now, but the shrine at Caversham and the relics of Reading Abbey together once ranked alongside Walsingham and Santiago de Compostela for their sanctity, and both attracted hordes of pilgrims.

The shrine of Our Lady of Caversham was known to several pious Kings and Queens of England, and must have been well established as a focus for devotions in the eleventh century, when it is first recorded in historical documents. Its power of attraction was substantially increased by gifts of religious relics and precious metals and jewels from a number of devout patrons. Amongst their number was Agnes Giffard, widow of the Duke of Buckingham who, in 1106, gave the shrine a piece of iron brought back from the Crusades by Robert, Duke of Normandy — a battle companion of her late husband. This wasn't just any old iron, however; it was believed by the faithful to be part of the spear which pierced the side of Jesus of Nazareth on the cross. In 1238-39 Henry III ordered oaks to be provided from his royal forests so that boats could be built to transport the ever-increasing numbers of pilgrims across the River Thames from Reading Abbey to Caversham. In 1241 Henry donated a massive 4lb candle and 1500 tapers to light the effigy of the Virgin Mary which stood in the shrine. The effigy was by then a magnificent sight, being a life-size wooden statue covered in gold and wearing a heavy gold crown created from the donation of 20lb of broken gold pieces by Isobel, Countess of Warwick; she also provided silver cloth and precious stones for its adornment. Other relics, which exerted such a spellbinding influence on the medieval mind, were a part of the alleged Holy Halter with which Judas hanged himself and the dagger which had killed Eadward the Martyr in Corfe Castle in 979. The shrine was a centre of healing, and pilgrims would come to hang up wax tokens of body parts, praying for cures for those afflicted with disease and infirmities.

The effigy was by then a magnificent sight being a life-size wooden statue covered in gold and wearing a heavy gold crown

On 17 July 1532 Henry VIII's wife Catherine of Aragon made her last pilgrimage to the shrine as a Queen, and shortly afterwards lost her position when Henry divorced her and declared his religious revolution and personal war against the Pope and Roman Catholicism. In 1538, on the orders of Henry's henchman Thomas Cromwell, a Dr John London arrived in Caversham to destroy the shrine and its relics. So completely was this task accomplished that its site has never been truly re-discovered. Dr London's report to Cromwell makes chilling reading, in the style of an enthusiastic ethnic cleansing operation:

> '*In my most humble manner I have me commendyd unto yower gude Lordeschippe, a certenyng the same that I have pullyd down the image of our ladye at Caversham whereunto wasse great pilgrimage. The image ys platyd over with silver and I have putt yt in a cheste fast lockyd and nayld uppe, and by the next bardge that comythe from Reding to London yt shall be brought to your lordeschippe. I have also pullyd down the place sche stode in with all other ceremonyes as lightes, schrowdes, crowchys, and imagies of wex, hanging about the chapell, and have defacyd the same thorowly in exchuyng of any farther resortt thedyr.*'

Upon what occult foundations were built the supernatural spots that humanity calls sacred in all cultures all over the world? Just how did these *genii loci* arise? Through eons of ancestor worship, homages to sky gods and earth mothers, the sprites and spirits of nature, tentative Celtic and Roman Christianity followed by the post-Reformation blitzkrieg of many-headed Protestantism and nonconformity; just where did it all start? What were the sources of these foundations? Visions are documented, as are telepathic messages; water divinities certainly are conjured up as well as healing springs, caves, sacred trees and mountains. In a supernatural topography there are certain basic themes simply added to, overlaid and transmogrified through time. At Caversham the original sacred spot was possibly a spring or a cave, or a spring issuing from a cave. Nobody will now know for sure. What is certain is that there was a pagan sacred spring because it was Christianised into St Anne's Well; a make-over from the Celtic. St Ann or Anne herself is not mentioned *at all* in the Bible, although she was deemed to be the mother of the Blessed Virgin Mary some centuries later. Her addition to the ranks of Saints seems to have been mysterious or just downright political. Pope Urban VI popularised the royal wedding plans of Richard II and *Anne* of Bohemia, for instance, by giving strict instructions to the faithful that they should 'big up' (*biggus uppus* in Monty Python Latin) 26 July, the Feast Day of St Ann... and we thought spin was just a modern political institution.

P is for PITT DIAMOND

Whenever stories of mega-wealth emerge the immediate reaction of most people is to imagine what crime or trick has been perpetrated to acquire so much cash so quickly. The shameful slave trade that created many of the nouveau riche of the eighteenth-century British establishment is well documented. The many industrial and landed dynasties that were founded at this time, with the obscene profits based on the 'triangular trade' in slaves, tobacco, alcohol, sugar, spices and coffee, are still with us, although now these original sins are barely noticed and never mentioned. Amidst this imperial plunder lies the story of the so-called Pitt Diamond and its one-time owner, the man destined to become known as 'Diamond Pitt'.

The story has its origins in India, at the Parteal diamond mines on the north bank of the Kistna River, where rough diamonds were deposited in water-borne alluvium from a decomposed diamondiferous source. Although some rough diamonds look at this stage like dirty marbles, it was easy to spot the potential big ones as they emerged from the dust and dirt. Slave or indentured labour was used to extract these gems. The opportunities to remove a diamond by the workforce were few as armed overseers and guards exerted a terrible vengeance on

Pitt opted to secrete it at Stratfield Saye as he deemed it a safer location than the Bank of England!

any transgressions on behalf of the mine-owners. Stealing undoubtedly ended with beatings and deaths. So it was with the cursed story of the 'Pitt Diamond'. In 1701 a slave worker whose name is unrecorded by history allegedly discovered a massive rough diamond in the diggings. Thinking quickly, he cut his leg open with a sharp tool, gouged a hole in the flesh, and before binding up his profusely bleeding wound inserted the dirty diamond under a flap of skin. Thus bandaged into a bloody cavity in his flesh, the diamond and slave miner made their way out of the mine and escaped detection. Knowing that this ugly pebble represented his ticket to freedom, the slave managed to get aboard a ship in the harbour. Here he ill-advisedly shared his story with an unscrupulous English captain in return for a passage out of India. This was his death warrant, and according to legend he was either murdered on board the boat in the harbour or simply thrown overboard en route to Bombay. A great Indian diamond dealer called Jamchund bought the stone from the captain, but in 1702 offered it for sale at 200,000 pagodas (c £100,000) to Thomas Pitt who, when he was not shipping opium, was on the lookout for large diamonds. The

asking price was brought down by several months of Pitt's haggling, aided by his ally Daniel Benyon and the diamond eventually changed hands for 48,000 pagodas (c £24,000).

Pitt sent the rough stone, of possibly 410-426 carats and the largest known diamond in the world, to England with his son John, under strict instructions as to how to care for it and smuggle it through customs. In London it went to a Mr Cope, who offered the promise that when cut it would be 'the wonder of the world'. It was turned into a 140.5 carat brilliant cut measuring approximately 32 × 34 × 25mm, leaving many other large pieces which were valued at £7000. The cutting took a nervous two years and cost about £500, and the smaller stones were sold to Peter the Great of Russia. The principal gem, which has only a slight imperfection, is considered to be one of the most brilliant of the world's known large diamonds, and Pitt had hoped to flog it to English royalty; but he had to wait fifteen years for a wealthy buyer. During this time Pitt opted to secrete it at Stratfield Saye as he deemed it a safer location than the Bank of England! In 1717 Pitt, then 64 and worried by his gout, sold the gem to Philip II, Duke of Orleans and Regent of France, for £130,000. Pitt smuggled the great diamond into France himself accompanied by two sons and a son-in-law for security, using a concealed space in the enlarged heel of one of his boots.

In 1797 the gem was pawned for the cash that helped Napoleon come to power, and was then fitted to his coronation sword in 1804

Since that time it has been known as the *Regent Diamond*. It became part of the crown that Louis XV wore at his coronation in 1723; Marie Antoinette later borrowed it to form the centrepiece of a large black velvet hat which she flounced about in to great impact, but it may have ultimately contributed to her downfall as the French peasantry starved. During the early phases of the French Revolution, as royals were losing their heads, France also 'lost' many of the royal treasures, including the Regent and French Blue diamonds, when the Garde Meuble (Royal Treasury) was ransacked in 1792. Some of the gems were soon recovered, but the Regent could not at first be traced. It was later found hidden in a Parisian house. In 1797 the gem was pawned for the cash that helped Napoleon come to power, and was then fitted to his coronation sword in 1804. Marie Louisa, Napoleon's second wife, carried the Regent to the Chateau of Blois and then to Austria to hide it when he was exiled to Elba in 1814. Later, her father returned it to France. In 1825 the Regent was displayed by Charles X at his coronation, but by the time of Napoleon III it was made into a piece of jewellery for Empress Eugenie. Following this it just managed to escape the tawdry auction of the French Crown Jewels in 1887 and became part of an exhibition at the Louvre. On the Nazi invasion of France and the capture of Paris it was posted out to the countryside to Chambord to be hidden. It is now back at the Louvre Museum and awaiting its next adventure into history.

Pitt's adventures ended in Swallowfield in 1726 when he died on the estate he had purchased in 1719 with his diamond money. He was not a well-liked man, and even his admirers speaking at his funeral service described him in forthright terms. Pitt the boy had gone to sea and ended up smuggling dodgy goods out of India like a maritime 'Del Boy'. He became a wanted man, stealing from under the noses of the East India Company monopoly. He was accused of being a pirate, law-suited, threatened and arrested, but in the end they tired of his determination and invited him into the company to become Governor of Fort George. He continued his aggressive behaviour towards others (described as having a 'haughty, huffing, dazing temper') and he even lambasted his own cousin John Pitt as being 'crack-brained'. However, the vast profits from the diamond had enabled Pitt to buy not only Swallowfield but also the huge Cornish estate at Boconnoc for £50,000 from the widow of Lord Mohun, who had been killed in a duel. He acquired several other properties at the same time. It was at Swallowfield that he later allegedly received visitations from the shade of the murdered Indian slave worker who had found the diamond in the first place, a ghost of 'a black man that walks the Queen Anne's Gallery'. Pitt was clearly a determined creature, driven by money lust and the desire to travel further than the station given to him by birth as the second son of a rural rector in Dorset, albeit one whose grandfather had been Clerk of the Exchequer to Elizabeth I. That he achieved his ambition is clear, and in so doing spawned generations of Pitts imbued with much the same determination, albeit through slippery politics rather than slippery commerce: William Pitt the Elder (1708-1778), Whig statesman (for whom Pittsburgh, USA was named); and Pitt the Younger (1759-1806) who became Britain's youngest-ever Prime Minister.

is for QUEER THINGS (VARIOUS)

Did you know that if you draw a circle centred next to Silbury Hill in Wiltshire, Europe's largest prehistoric man-made mound, you can connect the enigmatic little pond that marks the meeting point of Hampshire, Berkshire and Wiltshire with Stonehenge, Uffington and Westbury White Horses, and Lambourn's Seven Barrows? Not many people know that.

Not well known either is the apocryphal old story of a Maidenhead publican who discovered that some ruffian bargemen were intent on raiding his larder and, having recently acquired some drowned puppies in a sack, decided to make a pie of them in anticipation of the raid. The puppy pie was duly stolen as predicted and apparently scotched away to be eaten near Marlow Bridge, where its gourmet trenchermen believed they were eating rabbit. Naturally this was long before Rolf Harris and his RSPCA TV series, but the story still attracts interest from North Korean tourists.

The World's most famous apple, the Cox's Orange Pippin, is a Berkshire product, although only by a freak of local government boundary reorganisation from its former residency in Surrey and Buckinghamshire.

In the film of the J.K. Rowling book *Harry Potter and the Philosopher's Stone* the sequence of filming involving the muggles' house at 4 Privet Drive, where Harry lived as a boy before his adventures at Hogwarts School, was taken in Bracknell. The magical excitement of a suburban housing estate in Martin's Heron was chosen after a nationwide trawl for suitable places. Harry's house is in fact 12 Picket Post Close.

A suburban housing estate in Martin's Heron was chosen after a nationwide trawl for suitable places. Harry's house is 12 Picket Post Close

Many of the outdoor scenes in *Carry on Camping*, starring Barbara Windsor and Sid James amongst many others, were filmed in Windsor Great Park, as were, in 2001, parts of the scenes featuring Angelina Jolie as 'Lara Croft' storming through the steamy Cambodian jungle in the film *Tomb Raider*.

Important parts of *Chariots of Fire* (1981) and *The Madness of King George* (1994) were set in the quad and buildings of Eton College.

Is there something strange in your neighbourhood? This parody of the song from the film *Ghostbusters* might seem quite apt and appropriate for parts of Padworth. Outwardly, the straggling village is a serene area peeping over the rim of the shallow Kennet Valley, but there have been some reports of very strange things happening. There are the so-called 'spooklights' – glowing globs of light which seem to soundlessly swish along certain lanes and byways of Padworth by night. These have been seen on many occasions throughout the past few hundred years or so and, therefore cannot be classed as a purely modern aerial phenomenon. The old Parish Clerk from 1871 to 1911, a Mr Edward Hobbs, saw the nocturnal lights on many occasions skipping along an old drovers' road from Padworth to Reading. He described them as looking like lamps glowing with a yellowish hue and that there were two of them. This pair made quick progress, but when close to any watchers they simply disappeared from view, followed by a bizarre stillness. Similar lights have been observed in Marfa, Texas and the Burton Dassett Hills near Banbury, and were once associated with the short-lived rise of a religious cult in North Wales at the turn of the twentieth century. As the Burton Dassett area and North Wales are seemingly closely correlated with geological faults a theory, so far unproven, has developed that these 'lights' are brief flickerings of energy released from subterranean earth movements. Whether or not Padworth is similarly underlaid by a major geological fault, or whether this is a completely different paranormal phenomenon, is unclear.

There is also something very odd about Padworth Old Rectory, where in recent years stories have been told of young people (including a hard-headed Scottish graduate engineer working for Babtie in Shinfield) being held down in bed by forceful unseen entities, and of flitting figures caught in car headlights.

Luckily, he wrote his autobiography before he was stuffed

On one occasion such a figure was seemingly run down by a vehicle entering the drive to the house. The driver was so convinced he had accidentally run someone over that he got out and conducted a search for the body. There was neither body nor damage to the car. The 'accidents' and attempted bed pressings have been laughed off as 'just' poltergeist activity. Is this simply a strange coincidence? But why Padworth?

And finally, in a dusty glass case at Slough Station is a stuffed dog standing upright on all fours wearing a little leather money-pouch on his back. This is the celebrated 'Station Jim' or 'Jim the Dog' who, if only he could talk, would have a splendid tale to tell. Luckily, he wrote his autobiography before he was stuffed. He arrived at the station as a tiny fluffy puppy, but the staff soon taught him to climb the steps of the footbridge, play roll-over-and-die, stand upright on his hind legs, sit up and beg, play leap-frog with small boys, and

extinguish dropped lighted matches with his foot. He could also sit in a chair wearing a cap with a pipe in his mouth. Jim's greatest talent, however, was to bark every time anyone approached him with a coin, because his job at the station was to collect money from passengers for the GWR Widows' and Orphans' Fund. Although Jim's career was tragically short he collected over £40 for the fund between 1894 and 1896, a remarkable amount of money at the time, which included at least one gold half sovereign. Jim took himself off on a number of train trips to Paddington and Windsor seeking more contributions, and once went as far as Leamington. Sadly, Jim died on 19 November 1896, still wearing his money-pouch, and his many railway friends decided to show their gratitude by having him stuffed. Bizarre but true.

R is for RELICS

On Caversham Bridge there is a tablet built into the ferroconcrete which describes how a number of religious relics were brought to Reading by '*an Angel with only one wing*'. This curious event does not seem to have a counterpart anywhere else in myth or legend; angels, even fallen ones, always have a pair of wings apiece... so what should we make of it? There is a possibility that it was a broken statue of an angel, which was a fairly common Christian religious icon of the time, converted into a reliquary or as housing for some particles of the great medieval trade in holy relics.

Reading was a boom town for relics... and a Mecca for pilgrims, simply because the Abbey acted as a well-endowed relic repository of magical paranormal healing and impromptu miracles. The preposterous gullibility of folk was fed by their gigantic faith in these objects, although it took another 800 years for the NHS to be invented and a new faith in medical science to be established, with X-rays and bottles of pills becoming the new miraculous cure-all concept. Back in the days of wingless or winged angels the relics list held at the Abbey boggles the mind. Chief amongst the treasures was the foreskin or prepuce of Jesus Christ which Henry I bestowed upon the Abbey; it had previously been in the possession of the Emperor Constantine. After that came bottles of blood and water from Jesus at the crucifixion, a gilded cross offered to him, a piece of his shoe and some stones and dirt from Bethlehem. Some of the BVM's hair and parts of her bed mingled with bits of Aaron's and Moses' rods, manna from Mount Sinai, and even the rock (part thereof) that Moses struck with his rod (before it fell apart). There was, very significantly, the whole hand of St James the Great, and a huge number of bony body parts of saints including Simeon, Thomas, Luke (tooth), Andrew (finger only but with bits of his cross), Philip (skull), Mary Magdalen, Pancras (arm bone), Quinton, David, Eadward the Martyr, Jerome, Stephen, Blaise, Osmund, Aethelwold (jawbone), Leodegarius, Herefrith, Margaret, Arnulf, Agnes, Frideswide and Anne. Not forgetting a scrap of St Ursula's coat.

The pilgrim trade was big business in medieval Reading with two centres to focus on, not only the Abbey and its relics but also the Caversham shrine. In the Premier Division of European pilgrimage sites were − after the Holy Land itself − Rome, Santiago de Compostela, Walsingham, Canterbury and Reading.

Henry I had a big hand (as it were) in creating Reading's eminence, as it was he who obtained and bestowed the alleged mummified hand of St James on the town's abbey.

St James was seemingly a well-travelled saint: he, with his brother John, despite being the simple sons of Zebedee, fishermen from Lake Galilee, were called upon by Jesus to be his 'sons of thunder'. They were awarded this title after threatening to destroy an inhospitable hamlet by calling down fire from heaven. It was tough love in those days. James was eventually martyred by Roman puppet king Herod Agrippa I, but not before he apparently wandered off to spend a few years preaching in the Spanish end of the Roman Empire before returning to Jerusalem and a willing martyr's death. Weirdly perhaps, his body was taken to the Mediterranean Sea and put into a *stone boat*. This peculiar heavier-than-water 'boat' was then whisked away by angels in a wind and landed at Padron on North West Spain's rocky Atlantic coast. From here it was dragged inland by local Queen Lupa's oxen to be buried in a marble tomb. Then it was forgotten for 800 years or so until a hermit was led to it in a vision. Strangely, at that time Spain was suffering from a periodic Saint shortage and desperately needed someone hefty to counteract the religious powers of the Moors pouring in from Africa. Amazingly, as soon as the local bishop clapped his eyes on the bones he declared – obviously without the need for DNA analysis – the remains to be unequivocally those of the great St James. Great news for one and all: Spain saved and lucrative tourist trade created in one afternoon. The pilgrims came in droves and (appropriately) used drovers' roads all across Europe to get to Santiago de Compostela by funnelling like migrating birds into narrow channels to cross through the Pyrenees and then over Spain's deserts to the Land's End of Galicia, the province of Finisterre. After visiting the saint's bones they would journey to the sea at Padron and pick scallop shells off the beach to carry back home on their reverse journey as visible signs of their completed pilgrimage. Which is why, when Henry acquired the blessed hand of St James and gave it to Reading Abbey, the town also inherited the three scallop shells that are still visible today on the coat of arms of Reading University. The scallop of the pilgrims is also used today on the waymarks and signposts of the long distance walking routes to Santiago through France and Spain.

is for SWAN UPPING

If you visit New Zealand on holiday it is not impossible that your hospitable and generous hosts will sit you down to a dinner of roast swan or swan burgers. Bizarrely enough it is not only possible but tacitly encouraged to kill, cook and eat swans in that lovely country, albeit under licence and when in season. Indeed, the Australian Black Swan is classified as a pest or, to give the feast its scientific justification, an Invasive Non-Native Species. A delicious recipe for a warm salad of smoked swan breast over taglialini-style leeks, with seared pineapple and feta with truffle oil vinaigrette was broadcast on Radio New Zealand by chef John Clarke in 2006. Swan meat has been described as tasting like mutton with a pleasant hint of fishy gaminess.

You are highly unlikely to hear the expression 'throw another swanee on the barbie mate' here in England though, unless you uniquely belong to one of the Cambridge colleges or live near the River Nene in Peterborough. In St John's College the Fellows have the ancient privilege granted by the monarch to eat swan at High Table. Her Majesty the Queen can also place a take-away order for swan, as can the Worshipful Company of Dyers and the Worshipful Company of Vintners. In Peterborough, however, the alleged unscrupulous eating of swans by homeless Eastern European migrant workers has reached the pages of the Daily Mail, even if it does not yet appear on the menu at local restaurants. A couple of hundred years ago such an offence carried the penalty of transportation to the antipodes or, earlier still, death by hanging. Obviously the reason for this degree of royal protection is that swans are good to eat and officially regarded as an important food source and designated as such since the twelfth century. Swans were often prepared as the centrepiece of a banquet and very dramatic ways of cooking the swan body, gilding it and serving it with the reserved feathered head, neck and wings were attempted by medieval cooks.

This is a remnant of catching swans for cooking

In Berkshire, however, we do Swan Upping; and we do it properly. The slightly bizarre ritual takes place on the Berkshire portion of the river Thames every year, usually in the third week of July when the young swans (cygnets) are about two months old. This is a remnant of catching swans for cooking, although the monarch no longer regularly eats swan meat but keeps the right alive as a form of Droit de Seigneur by rounding up the mute swans on part of the Thames. The Uppers are assembled to carry out their solemn duties on behalf of the Queen, the Vintners and the Dyers, and are led by the Master of the Queen's Swans.

Upping is a form of stocktaking for the *virtual* royal menu or for use as gifts for special events. To conserve the birds, prior to the introduction of turkeys (as an alternative to swan meat) only the royal household had the right to own them, but in 1472 the Vintners were granted a Royal Charter and in 1482 so were the Dyers. Since then the Uppers have gathered on the river in their randans (flat-bottomed rowing boats) and skiffs, in their scarlet, green and blue jackets embroidered with silver badges proclaiming their status such as 'Her Majesty's Swan Keeper' or 'Vintners Royalty' to catch cygnets, ring some of them on the leg or legs with an ID tag (formerly the Uppers used to mark their beaks with penknives), record their parentage and drink toasts.

The Queen appoints both a Swan Marker and the Queen's Swan Warden. In 2011 David Barber was Swan Marker and Professor Christopher Perrins the Swan Warden. The five-day trip up the Thames from Sunbury to Abingdon, with royal pennants flying at the stern, is a colourful but hard-working operation, starting at nine in the morning and ending at six each day. In recent years many swans on the Thames have died due to being caught in fishing lines or injured by hooks, and previously some were poisoned after ingesting lead shot weights discarded by anglers. Lead has now been banned, but wanton vandalism by bad lads with air rifles and catapults is a constant worry. Even more concerning is the spread of a deadly virus called duck enteritis that has killed over 100 swans on the Windsor Reach alone with many more breeding pairs weakened by the severe winter cold. The assessment of swan health is therefore an important part of the census task, and all cygnets are weighed and measured. In keeping with the ancient tradition all non-royal cygnets are ringed to declare ownership; the Vintners ring both legs and the Dyers just one. All the Queen's swans remain un-ringed

In 2009 Her Majesty the Queen made history by attending the Swan Upping in person for the first time, and indeed she was the first reigning monarch for many centuries to attend the ritual event. It's not recorded what was for lunch.

T is for TUTTIMEN OF HUNGERFORD

At some point in our past there must have been a reason to celebrate Hocktide just as much as there was to enjoy Yuletide. Easter, which is of course the pagan festival of spring and the rebirth of nature (Eostre), is a moveable feast in that it follows the lunar cycle rather than a set pattern of months and fixed dates. Just as Easter Day can fall anytime between 22 March and 25 April, so Hocktide follows a week after Easter Sunday on the Monday and Tuesday. It has some of the characteristics of April Fool's Day with elements of misrule and anarchy, but also something hinting slightly towards sex (and bondage!)... maybe a second-chance festival for those unlucky not to have conceived earlier in spring, when creating new life might have been seen as a sacred act. The meaning of the bizarre Hocktide Monday practice of the men tying up the women before releasing them for a 'kiss', and reversing the bondage role on the Tuesday when the women demand money from the men, a function of the ceremony called 'binding', is lost to obscurity. You can invent your own contemporary versions of this if you wish. Nobody knows for sure what the 'hock' of Hocktide means, unless there are hidden links to certain German wines or horse anatomy. However, Hocktide has been persistent in English folklore and celebrated in a number of places including Coventry and villages in Hertfordshire, although the original sense of the ceremony has been lost.

> The bizarre Hocktide Monday practice of the men tying up the women before releasing them for a 'kiss', and reversing the bondage role on the Tuesday when the women demand money from the men

Hocktide celebrations have been thought by some historians to commemorate the massacre of the Danes by Ethelred the Unready in a bloody pogrom against all people of Danish origin in the southern, Saxon part of the Danelaw, the division across England from the Severn estuary to the Humber. This rash action ultimately led to severe reprisals against the Saxons and the ruinous imposition of fines by the incensed Danes. The northern Danelaw neighbours were doubly aggrieved by the public beheading of a Danish princess and the bloodthirsty slaughter of all her children. The other Danish context might have been a celebration of the death of Harthacanute in the eleventh century.

However, Hocktide cannot be the acknowledged derivative of these events, because the dates do not match: the massacre took place on 13 November 1002 and Harthacnut died on 8 June 1042.

The greatest living remnant of an amended Hocktide ceremony in Britain today occurs at Hungerford in Berkshire when the Tuttimen gather. It is wrapped up in another local celebration, that of John O'Gaunt's alleged granting to the townspeople, in the fourteenth century, of common rights of fishery in the river Kennet from Irish Stile to Eldren Stub. All written records of this grant have been lost (although for some peculiar reason a battered brass horn was cited as proof positive that the grant had been given). With fat trout to be had by the townspeople for free, the issue became a legal struggle with the principal landowners, the Duchy of Lancaster, for centuries. The issue was not finally settled until James I granted rights in Hungerford to two Londoners in March 1612. Eventually, five years later, these were flogged off to the Constable and thirteen other people as trustees of the townspeople on 16 June 1617. The houses that these trustees lived in or owned in 1617 have retained the rights to the present day, and any living occupier is therefore a modern commoner and representative of this historic lineage.

A battered brass horn was cited as proof positive that the grant had been given

Although the granting of rights is unrelated to Hocktide, the two strands have become somewhat confusingly but entertainingly entwined. On Hocktide Tuesday or Tutti-Day, the modern Hungerford commoners meet to hold court. At this event they deal with all matters associated with the administration of the common, the common rights, including the rare right of piscary to fish the river Kennet, and grazing. Fines are imposed upon those common right holders who fail to attend the court. The election of officers to manage the common for the year is held. Among the court officials are the Constable, the Port Reeve, the Bailiff, eight Water-Bailiffs, eight Overseers of the Common, three Keepers of the Keys of the Common Coffer, two Ale-Tasters and four Tutti-men. Their duties are both commonsense and obscure, perhaps reflecting the mingling of traditions from the earlier Hocktide festivals with the granting of common rights. The Bellman calls the commoners to the court by blowing an ancient horn called the Lucas Horn at 8 a.m.

On the High Street the big Tutti-Day parade begins. Two Tutti-men dressed in top hat and tails armed with stout sticks called Tutti Poles, surmounted by flowers and an orange studded with cloves, are required to visit all 102 proper-ties in the town to which common rights are attached. They are followed by the Orange Man or Orange Scrambler with his weird be-feathered hat and a white sack containing oranges. The Tutti wenches have the most popular role as they give out oranges in return for a kiss or a penny in a seemingly straightforward reference to the Hocktide 'binding' element. Not to be outdone, the two Tutti-Men demand a kiss or a penny from the female representatives of each of the 102 properties before giving them an orange (and all in the best possible taste, with euphemisms excluded). An ambulance containing a quart of lip salve and ice-packs will no doubt be included in all future cavalcades. At the end there is a Hocktide Lunch with its *Plantagenet Punch,* an ale-tasting using large pewter jugs. Newcomers (formerly new commoners, presumably) are initiated in a mock horse-shoeing display called 'Shoeing the Colts'. The children of the town used to gather before the town hall steps to be showered with sweets, which replaced the former practice of throwing pennies heated over hot coals at them... suffer little children. Now, because of traffic dangers, this quaint practice has been dropped.

is for UFOs (and IFOs?)

Windsor Castle, August 1783

The world's first aquatint etching of a UFO was created by Paul Sandby, a Royal Academician and painter of repute, following a remarkable incident at Windsor in 1783; or was it merely an identified flying object or IFO, in this case a meteor? Following the arrival of the Age of Reason, the establishment of Science and the scientific way, men of letters would gather together under Royal patronage. These men, and those who formed the Royal Society of Arts and Commerce (RSA) in 1662 (encouraged by the restored monarchy of Charles II) were exploring everything in the known universe and pioneering new understanding of how everything worked. However, Science and the Arts would still come together to debate issues of the day, and on one such occasion on the North Terrace of Windsor Castle the following luminaries were gathered: Tiberius Cavallo, Thomas Sandby, Dr James Lind, Dr Lockman and two unknown ladies. 18 August was to become an interesting day, for as they talked and walked at around 9 p.m, a most profound event took place in the sky over the Thames Valley.

What they witnessed was described in words by those present and transcribed into history long before Boeing 777s and Airbus A380s were invented to plague the modern inhabitants of Windsor Castle. The description could well grace any modern UFO report, such was its quality. However, because of the presence of Royal Academy artist Thomas Sandby there also exists an etching of the event produced by Thomas and his brother Paul, which captures an eyewitness perspective of the movements in the sky that fateful day. There are two explanations for this event: the first and most widely accepted is that it was a very rare but spectacular 'bright meteor'; the second that it was a UFO. Whatever it was, it had multiple witnesses the length of Britain, including at least one more artistic rendition, now in the British Museum, by a schoolmaster called Henry Robinson from Winthorpe near Newark on Trent. The event also stimulated an offer to collect evidence from eyewitnesses by Royal Society member Charles Blagden. He presented a report to the RSA in the following year. Cavallo's own account is also reported in the Philosophical Transactions of the Royal Society. The Windsor

Blagden estimated its size as half a mile across. If it was a meteor it is not known where it came to earth or where its impact crater lies

witnesses saw flashes of light on the northern horizon, then a roundish shiny object which they sized as half the width of the moon. It was almost stationary in the sky and bluish in colour, but soon began to move and grew very much brighter and ascended above the horizon in an oblique eastward direction. At this moment the object was oblong, and so bright that it illuminated the whole landscape. It developed a tail and then multiplied into several small luminous bodies, each with its own tail. After this brief change of direction it turned itself to travel along the horizon before the light decreased abruptly, and it disappeared at a point south-east of their observations. Ten minutes later a rumbling noise was heard. In Blagden's report, collated from numerous observers from Shetland to Brussels, the luminous sphere became elliptical and kept varying between the two. It was directly over General Murray at Blair House, Blair Atholl, as it passed south-south-east. Over the Yorkshire-Lincolnshire borders it diverted to the east but produced a cluster of smaller glowing bodies or ovals. The assemblage then moved south-eastwards towards Suffolk before returning to a SSE course over Essex, passed over Folkestone in Kent and thence across Dover Straits to Dunkirk and onwards. The speed of the object was estimated at 20 miles per second and its height guesstimated around 58 miles; it seems to have had a tail throughout, but this was seen by some as a spiral. Blagden mentions that instead of exploding and vanishing the object became more compact, or perhaps the fragments reunited. He also notes that the object, unlike other reported meteors, was not descending towards the earth but moving parallel with it. There was no sound associated with it in Scotland, but elsewhere some observers heard a hissing, whizzing or crackling noise. Blagden estimated its size as half a mile across. If it was a meteor it is not known where it came to earth or where its impact crater lies.

He took his thermos out of his fishing bag for a cup of tea. As he looked about him, a luridly bright light appeared in the sky

Basingstoke Canal, Aldershot, August 1983

Not far south of the Berkshire-Surrey border, on the night of 12-13 August 1983 Alfred Burtoo, a 77-year-old pensioner, was sitting by the side of the Basingstoke Canal in Aldershot doing some fishing, with his dog Tiny tied to an umbrella stick next to him. His favourite spot for tench (and the occasional big carp) was about 115 yards north of the Gasworks Bridge on Government Road, and at about 1.15 a.m. he took his thermos out of his fishing bag for a cup of tea. As he looked about him, a luridly bright light appeared in the sky over North Town, roughly to the south of his position. The light hovered, then wobbled in a 'falling leaf' motion over the railway lines before seeming to descend on the other side of the canal opposite the REME base, whereupon most of the lights went out. Perplexed, but not afraid, the old soldier and former Canadian bear hunter lit a cigarette; then Tiny began to growl. Suddenly, within five feet of the fishing spot, were two four-foot-high humanoid 'forms' dressed in pale green one-piece suits with green helmets blacked out at the front. One beckoned for Alfred to follow him; so all three set off down the path towards the bridge, where the green forms *melted* through the railings whilst Alfred had to clamber over. They crossed Government Road and scrambled down the other side onto the towpath, where a 40-50-foot-wide object jutted out over the canal supported on 'ski runners' with a set of steps leading to the ground. All three entered the craft, which looked like seamless burnished aluminium on the outside and black metal on the inside. It was dimly lit and octagonal with a central shaft with a Z-shaped handle. Two other forms in identical dress were also in the machine. No other controls, knobs, buttons or bolts were to be seen, but there was a faint smell of decaying meat. Alfred was then told to stand under an amber light next to a wall for ten minutes or so before he was asked his age. He was then peremptorily told 'You can go. You are too old and infirm for our purpose'. Alfred retraced his steps and saw the object begin to rise with its porthole lights fully on and a hum like an electric generator before it zapped off at high speed over the military cemetery. He was very reluctant to inform the press because he imagined his wife would refuse to let him go night fishing!

Although these bizarre events are 200 years apart almost to the day, the nature of such aerial phenomena continues to confound science and tease our logical faculties. Who knows what is going on out there? You decide: IFOs or UFOs?

V is for VICAR OF BRAY

Political satire is often the cruellest wit, but frequently the most appreciated by the general populace as it exposes the hypocrisy of governments, religious leadership and those who would put themselves above others. The great tragi-comedic plays of Shakespeare such as *Measure for Measure* explore such human frailties, often with very public put-downs. The fact that we are still hearing the message of such works today unfortunately reassures us that this is an enduring theme in life; the foibles of the high and mighty are the same as those of the lowly and weak and are continuous throughout the history of human civilisation, like some form of psychological archetype. This tendency towards hypocrisy seems to be attendant on every human society based on hierarchy, rank, privilege and class distinctions. Sadly, we never seem to learn from the past. Much as Shakespeare used the Elizabethan playhouses to make a point, so today we use television and other mass media. Indeed, who amongst the middle-aged today will ever forget the cringeworthy satirical put-downs by Spitting Image of Margaret Thatcher's government and Neil Kinnock's opposition party members, and the cruelly unforgettable Roy Hattersley puppet. More recently, the spiky cartoons of Steve Bell that portrayed Tony Blair as goggle-eyed and big-eared, or David Cameron as Little Lord Fauntleroy and Nick Clegg as Pinocchio, carry on the history of attempted satirical assassination.

The benighted, amoral creature that was the 'Vicar of Bray' thus became an enduring symbol of hypocrisy celebrated not by cartoon or theatre but by song. Satirists will turn their inventive wit to any medium to get the point over. The amazing success of these tactics ensures that even when later generations have no recollection of the circumstances or the context we still 'get it' today. The Vicar of Bray in Berkshire has thus become a motif within the English-speaking world for arrant hypocrisy, but tracking down the original incumbent of the position is not an easy matter. There are a number of potential candidates; the only 'evidence' we have is contained in the words of the satirical song, but there are several versions of it. It seems likely that the words of the original were adapted to suit later circumstances. The most commonly understood version today corresponds to the shifting political sands of the seventeenth and eighteenth centuries, but the original might be from the lethal period of religious declaration in the time of Henry VIII.

> **The benighted, amoral creature that was the 'Vicar of Bray' thus became an enduring symbol of hypocrisy**

Between 1540 and 1588 the Vicar of Bray was Simon Aleyn who, if he wished to retain his living (and his life), had to alternate between the religious dogmas of Henry VIII, Edward VI, Mary Tudor and Elizabeth I and hypocritically subvert his own religious convictions. This was a time of great religious martyrs, and those who chose the route of religious conviction were frequently and very publicly burnt at the stake as heretics. It was not easy being a simple rural vicar during such times. This period might have seen the writing of the original version of the song.

On the other hand, Francis Carswell was Vicar of Bray for 42 years between 1667 and 1709 and lived through the tumultuous times of Charles II, James II and the unique shared reign of William and Mary following the 'Glorious' or 'bloodless' Revolution of 1688.

Another contender, proposed by the then Vicar of Bray in 1745, is Simon Simonds; but he was only a sixteenth-century canon at nearby Windsor, and not incumbent at Bray.

The version of the song that is most frequently remembered, and might have been created by a witty trooper in the army of George I, runs to a jaunty six verses with an intervening chorus. Here's a sample of it. (For those who are wondering what is described in verse three as a 'Cat in Pan', it is believed to be a type of pancake, therefore something easily flipped.)

In good King Charles's golden days
When Loyalty no harm meant;
A Zealous High-Church man I was,
And so I gain'd Preferment.
Unto my Flock I daily Preach'd,
Kings are by God appointed,
And Damn'd are those who dare resist,
Or touch the Lord's Anointed.

Chorus:
And this is law, I will maintain
Unto my Dying Day, Sir
That whatsoever King may reign,
I will be the Vicar of Bray, Sir!

When Royal James possest the crown,
And popery grew in fashion;
The Penal Law I shouted down,
And read the Declaration:

The Church of Rome I found would fit
Full well my Constitution,
And I had been a Jesuit,
But for the Revolution.

When William our Deliverer came,
To heal the Nation's Grievance,
I turn'd the Cat in Pan again,
And swore to him Allegiance;
Old Principles I did revoke,
Set conscience at a distance,
Passing Obedience is a Joke,
A Jest is non-resistance.

When Royal Ann became our Queen,
Then Church of England's Glory,
Another face of things was seen,
And I became a Tory:
Occasional Conformists base
I Damn'd, and Moderation,
And thought the Church in danger was,
From such Prevarication.

When George in Pudding time came o'er
And Moderate Men looked big, Sir,
My Principles I chang'd once more,
And so became a Whig, Sir.
And thus Preferment I procur'd
From our Faith's great Defender
And almost every day abjur'd
The Pope, and the Pretender.

The Illustrious House of Hannover,
And Protestant succession,
To these I lustily will swear,
Whilst they can keep possession:
For in my Faith, and Loyalty,
I never once will faulter,
But George, my lawful king shall be,
Except the Times shou'd alter.

is for WHIRLWINDS

When Isambard Kingdom Brunel planned his Great Western Railway from London to Bristol he was meticulous in the detail of the route, the gradient and the architecture, but what no-one could plan for was the capricious nature of Nature itself. Construction was delayed for nearly a year between Twyford and Reading by the unusually unstable sands that necessitated the vast Sonning Cutting to be re-graded and cut back again and again until a safe route to Reading could be achieved. Several navvies died in the attempt to stabilise these shifting post-glacial quicksands. Just when the great project was six days away from the completion of the line to Reading and the opening of the station, Nature once again vented her spleen at these earth-fiddling engineers. The victim this time was the unfortunate Henry West, a 24-year-old carpenter from Wilton in Wiltshire. West had been working on the final stages of the roof lantern on the top of the station when a violent storm of preposterous fury broke over Reading. On 24 March 1840 a whirlwind, a tornado as we might describe it today, struck the station and ripped off the lantern roof, taking young Henry with it. His dead body was recovered from a trench on the far side of the station 200 yards away from where he had been working. The shock and trauma of the event deeply affected his working colleagues who erected a simple wooden railway sleeper memorial as a mark of respect. In the mawkish doggerel of the time it read:

Sudden the change
I in a moment fell and had not time
To bid my friends farewell
Yet hushed be all complaint
tis sweet, tis blest
To change Earth's stormy scenes
For endless rest,
Dear Friends prepare,
Take warning by my fall,
So shall you bear with joy
Your Saviour's call.

An additional memorial can be seen in the graveyard of St Laurence's church in central Reading, originally erected by Henry West's brother in 1862, renewed by his great-niece in 1924 and latterly by Reading Corporation in 1971.

Tornados are generally viewed as weather phenomena that affect the mid-western states of the USA, often with lethal impacts and massive destruction. Most people know of the Wizard of Oz and how a whirlwind carried off Dorothy and her little dog Toto from Kansas to a land far away in the clouds. Well, Reading isn't exactly Kansas (although there is a town in Kansas called Reading that has tragically just had a fatal tornado) but the UK has recorded a surprisingly high number of tornados and marine waterspouts. These versions are minor in scale and impact compared to the USA, which has about 800 a year, but they are more frequent than might be imagined with data on between 30 and 50 per year collected by the UK tornado and storm research organisation TORRO.

Nature once again vented her spleen at these earth-fiddling engineers

Reading is no stranger to tornados; Sarah Davies, a weather advisor from the Met Office in the South East, reported to the BBC after one hit Chestnut Crescent, School Green, Shinfield in July 2007 and said 'As a country, tornados are actually quite common and happen more frequently per area in the UK than in the United States, although they are not as serious'. In 2009 Reading was hit by another tornado which struck the area around St Anne's Primary School in Caversham, causing damage to trees, buildings and walls.

There has also been a mysterious history of bizarre bangs and rumbles over Reading from the nineteenth century that could not be attributed to aircraft and occurred in clear skies without threat of thunderstorms. These odd noises persisted into the twentieth century and were heard across wide areas of Reading and its hinterland by many people. On 17 November 1905 something even more bizarre took place as a series of tremors were felt in the sky above Reading *at precise two hour intervals* from 11.30 a.m. to 3.30 p.m. The *Times* journalist who reported the event described it as 'the explosion of a meteorite, or bolide, high up in the atmosphere'... but this does not match the facts observed above Berkshire.

At 8 p.m. on 22 January 2011 two huge unexplained bangs in the sky rocked Haverhill, Suffolk and Saffron Walden and Thaxted in Essex, which are up to 13 miles apart. Shakes were felt in buildings and tremors in the ground. Furniture was also seen to move and windows heard to rattle. The British Geological Survey said that it was definitely *not* an earthquake, and the Fire Services checked to confirm that there were no supersonic military flights operating. The fire, police and other emergency services were called out to respond to frantic 999 calls from residents; but despite a rumour that an electricity sub-station had exploded, utility companies denied this was the case. No source for

the double explosion was ever found, and no debris or meteorite craters were discovered.

These thuds, bangs and rumbles from cloudless skies, like their kindred 'mystery hums', are a global phenomenon and are sometimes referred to as 'skyquakes' in the USA. The latest manifestations are being associated by some with the cause of the thousands of bird deaths in the USA in January 2011, when loud explosions in the sky 'like a cannon' were heard over many states and led to panic amongst the peacefully roosting birds. There is no currently agreed scientific explanation for them, although theories abound.

X is for X-ROADS

One day in 1920, when 65-year-old Alfred Watkins was riding out on business on his country horse, he had a sudden vision of a network of unseen 'lines' laid over the undulating landscape of his native Herefordshire. This started a line of thought (no pun intended) that still resonates today. Decades of topographical and historical research into the human forces that shaped the historic landscape followed this 'vision'. There are many who still follow through the lines that Alfred Watkins first described and are avidly scouring the world for things of a similar nature, such as the Nazca lines of Peru, the dragon lines or *lung mei* of China and the Inca Roads of South America.

When Watkins had consolidated his theories and tested some of them in the field and on the members of the Woolhope Naturalists' Field Club, he published a book called *The Old Straight Track* and thereby accidentally spawned the ley line industry, which has been revisited by some so that it fits with New Age theories about energy lines in the earth and dowsing. Watkins was very learned in ancient monuments, settlement place-names, byway and highway development, crossroads and five-ways, the positioning of churches, and cultural landscapes. He was knowledgeable about places as diverse as pre-Reformation London or deepest rural Monmouthshire. This polymath's ability to make lots of material connections caused considerable embellishment to his theory that early British peoples communicated by straight line tracks long before the 'invention' of the Roman Road. To prove his theory in the field Watkins was able to draw alignments of pre-Reformation churches, ancient cross-roads, Iron Age forts, Bronze Age tumuli and Stone Age long barrows, for instance, in straight line patterns which stretched for dozens of miles or in rare cases could be plausibly traced from Cornwall to the Norfolk coast. He then searched hard to expose hidden and unseen elements at certain nodal junctions along these lines such as completely buried mark-stones at ancient crossroads or undiscovered stone-bottomed fords where the leys crossed rivers. He invented theories connecting leys to modern transport routes and to patterns of trade, inviting the reader to consider further the significance of certain key place-name words which Watkins believed proved that certain commodities were carried along these leys in the past. He believed that place-names indicated connections with beacons

After death the bodies were left to rot and be devoured by carrion-eating birds or consumed by blowflies

and fire ceremonies at points on the ridges of hills where the leys crossed; he took photographs of mysterious notches cut onto skyline ridges precisely where the leys were drawn on his maps. Watkins was a no-nonsense materialist and a travelling tradesman, so he naturally preferred a cultural interpretation that not only seemed intuitively right to him but also suited his age of Empire when trade in goods and materials was global.

Two of Watkins's leys in Berkshire which you can test for your own curiosity are centred on Windsor Castle. You can also find a great sarsen mark-stone set into the house wall at the crossroads further west in Streatley.

Crossroads were also seen as places where gallows and gibbets were to be erected, perhaps as flamboyant warning symbols to the maximum number of the travelling public that crime does not pay. Gibbets, such as the one at bleak Combe high on the Berkshire Downs, were particularly dire forms of visual punishment: large metal lattice cages hung from chains from wooden cross-beams into which the guilty were poked with their heads clamped in place. This ensured that they could not lie down inside the cage to gain some respite from this torture by sleep but had to remain upright until dead through starvation, lack of water or exposure. After death the bodies were left to rot and be devoured by carrion-eating birds or consumed by blowflies.

Crossroads were regarded with some awe in former times, before scientific rationalism, as the points where portals to the other realms of spirit worlds might open up unexpectedly. These weaknesses in the fabric of material reality were to be crossed as quickly as possible, with a religious crossing of the heart and a murmur of a prayer to preserve one from evil. Such beliefs had a long history and a wide global reach from Greece to India and Java to Japan. On Walpurgis Nacht in Germany men would crack whips at crossroads to keep witches at bay. These beliefs even survive as modern myths, as in the story of Blues guitar legend Robert Johnson, who was said to have gained his musical talent from hanging around devil-frequented crossroads at night in the Mississippi delta. In ancient Greek mythology crossroads had their own goddess, Hecate, to whom offerings and sacrifices were made. Black Dogs, shucks or hellhounds such as that described by Sherlock Holmes in *The Hound of the Baskervilles* were the red-eyed night keepers of such places. In Bali food was left at crossroads to tempt demons out so they could be chased away by villagers.

Crossroads were seen as the places to bury the unconsecrated dead, perhaps as the location for a fast route to Hell. Holes were dug at the centre of the junction to bury suicides, for instance, or those executed as criminals. Other occupants, buried and hurriedly covered over, were those alleged to have the evil eye or to have exerted strange malign powers over their fellow beings... the usual suspects: witches and vampires, possibly the odd werewolf, indeed anyone deemed bizarre perhaps? All such deviants were done to death and quickly buried with a stake through the heart to pin them in place and avoid them cruising the after-life. Suicide was of course deemed to be a criminal act by the fact that people had 'murdered themselves' or *felo-de-se* as the law called it. Long before the latter-day curse of digging holes in the road to endlessly replace sewers, water and gas pipes, road traffic was held up by the burials of these unfortunates. One horse-and-carriage traffic jam in central London, at the place where Victoria Station is now, was created by the crowds watching the burial of a 22-year-old suicide, Abel Griffiths. This law student had killed his father after a 'depression in the brain' and his burial held up George IV in his carriage. The interment in a five-foot-deep pit of the still bloodied, unwashed body, wrapped in a winding sheet and still wearing his socks, dispensed with 'the disgusting part of the ceremony of throwing lime over the body and driving a stake through its heart'. The crowd that gathered there were indignant that the treatment of Griffiths was in stark contrast to another recent but noble suicide, that of Lord Castlereagh, the Marquis of Londonderry, in 1822. However in his case the law had been completely bent so that he could be buried in Westminster Abbey in great state. The moral and legal outrage created was allegedly the basis for a transformation in the law, and an Act of Parliament of 8 July 1823 (4 George IV c52) caused the practice of crossroad burials to cease... although suicides were only grudgingly buried in graveyards thereafter between 9 p.m. and midnight, without ceremony, and with the state taking everything they owned.

Y is for **YEMMERRAWANYEA, WARRU-LOONG AND WILLIE WIMMERA**

Yemmerrawanyea of the Eora tribe was just one of a very small group, a handful, of desperately sad aboriginal people imported as 'curiosities' from Australia to England in the eighteenth and nineteenth centuries. He arrived aboard the sailing ship *Atlantic* in 1793 and was exhibited in front of King George III, but a year later he was dead at the age of 19. Warru-loong, the 9-year-old son of a tribal chief, was brought to England in 1845 by the explorer Edward Eyre and presented to Queen Victoria in 1846, but left behind when Eyre departed to be Lieutenant-Governor of New Zealand. The boy was eventually apprenticed into a saddle-making firm in Birmingham in whose uncertain care he died of exposure in 1855, also aged 19. 'Willie' Wimmera was the youngest of the pitiful handful and died in Reading aged just 11.

The trade in transported convicts and felons in the opposite direction was equally sad and far more numerous and widespread. There was a small difference in circumstances; in England the charges that could get you transported for life were frequently trivial, and through the lens of modern sensibilities and jurisprudence seem very harsh, especially when children were involved. In the reverse direction, however, aborigines imported as curiosities were often the sole survivors of wanton massacres inflicted upon whole tribes whenever European settlers and natives happened to clash over land or other resources. The differences in legal niceties and the rule of law between continents was hardly an issue when the cruelties imposed on individuals were so numbing.

Willie Wimmera's bizarrely benighted life was short, and although it began in the wild outback bush of Wotjobaluk tribal aboriginal land it ended in Reading's London Road cemetery at plot 10, row A, section 44, half a world away from kith and kin. The tribe occupied ancestral lands around the Wimmera River in what was to become the Colony of New South Wales. In the mid-1830s early European explorers visited, mapped and reported back in what were the first stages of a complete take-over of all the best agricultural or mineral-rich landscapes, including the life-giving waters of the Wimmera River. As large numbers of sheep brought over by opportunistic settlers expanded over tribal lands, trouble between the two cultures expanded into wanton violence. In February 1846 a Wotjobaluk camp by the river was attacked, and as many of the tribe as possible were deliberately slaughtered by gun-toting settlers, including the Belgian Horatio Ellerman. It was alleged that Ellerman shot Willie's mother dead through the chest, but for some unknown reason spared the six-year-old

child. Willie's life did not improve and he simply became Ellerman's slave-worker at his home. In December 1850 Willie joined some men taking wood to Melbourne on a cart but became lost in the city. He fetched up in the company of some white children who took him home and fed him. Shortly afterwards 'Willie' was discovered by the Reverend Septimus Lloyd Chase.

The Reverend Chase had connections with St John's church in Reading, and as he was returning to England obviously thought that Willie should be educated and converted to the Christian faith. So Chase simply took him. The duo departed Melbourne on the barque *Sacramento* on 29 March 1851 with the boy described as a servant. On one day at sea *'he climbed to the mast-head, and said to the man stationed there "ver' near moon", and then descended on one rope'.*

It was not until September that they reached Reading via the Port of London. Here Willie was educated in writing by Chase's sister and evangelised by the Chase social circle, but he remained only two months in their company. *'There was but little evidence of a work of grace in his heart, and it was painful to see his want of gratitude, and frequent sullenness of temper'.*

He was packed off to a boys' school in Iver and taught to plait straw and make shoes. During his stay at Iver he fell ill with a pulmonary disease and came back to Reading for Christmas, but was boarded out with a motherly woman in a small terraced house on Orts Road. The Reverend

The differences in legal niceties and the rule of law between continents was hardly an issue when the cruelties imposed on individuals were so numbing

Chase got married in January 1852 at St Giles's Church, and whilst understandably distracted failed to notice that Willie's health was seriously declining. The Chases decided to send the boy back to Australia, but his condition worsened very quickly and he was baptised William Wimmera on his deathbed, to die a Christian death. The end came on 10 March 1852. Missionary Chase paid £3.3s for his private grave next to a pious African girl called Mary Smart.

The tragic postscript is that William Wimmera died not knowing that his father, brothers and other tribal members had survived the massacre. They in turn did not know that the Wotjobaluk 'Australian Boy' had lived on the other side of the Earth... until the story was translated to them by Moravian Christian missionaries who had been given a site for a congregational church on land in the Wimmera *graciously* donated by one newly rich landowner... called Horatio

Ellerman. In fact it was just another bitter sadistic act, because it was sacred land also used by the Wotjobaluk as their caribberie or corroborree ground where the dreamtime was sung and danced. The story of Willie came out during the confrontations that followed. One survivor said *'That was Jim Crow. I was with him when the white man's bullet killed his mother, down there near the bottom of the garden'*. Everyone then present visited Willie's mother's grave and said their piece. A year later the new church was built, and at the consecration were Jim Crow's father and the Reverend Lloyd Chase of Reading.

Z is for ZEBRA CROSSING (FIRST IN WORLD)

Leslie Hore-Belisha was Minister of Transport in 1934 and pressed hard for a Bill in Parliament to try to cut the appalling number of people killed by the relatively small number of motor vehicles then being driven on British roads. He is now remembered in the improbably named, and now somewhat incongruous, Belisha Beacon, the black and white striped poles topped with flashing orange globes erected by the side of pedestrian crossing points. Places to cross the road were at that time marked only by a series of almost invisible raised metal studs in the road surface. A few more tens of thousands of unfortunate road deaths later, in 1948, the Road Research Laboratory started playing with 1/24th scale models on its Lego set and also tried out different permutations of coloured road surface markings at 1000 different locations around the country. At the end of the tests, on 31 October 1951, the Ministry of Transport created the world's first official black and white striped crossing at Slough. Although nobody has been credited for certain with calling it the zebra crossing, there was a rumour that Jim Callaghan MP coined the term jokingly on a ministerial visit to the Road Research Lab in 1948, before the new designs were tested. When questioned in 1951, Callaghan couldn't recall saying it, so we might file the story under 'urban myth'.

This novelty solution to the pedestrian lottery of getting from A to B has survived for over 60 years, and stripes of black and white are still being painted onto road surfaces, albeit with newly attendant wiggly lines. The world's most famous zebra crossing was at Abbey Road in London close by the studios where many of the Beatles' greatest recordings were made, and was an instant hit when used as a cover photo feature of the successful album Abbey Road. However, in an act of flagrant cultural vandalism the original Abbey Road zebra

After the zebras, a whole Noah's Ark of animal street furniture erupted onto the road scenery with Pelicans, Puffins, Toucans...

crossing has been erased and a new one created further down the road in a sop to EU road safety bean-counters. Where are English Heritage when you need them most? As for the location of the world's first official zebra crossing in Slough... it was near the site of Boots the Chemists.

After the zebras, a whole Noah's Ark of animal street furniture erupted onto the road scenery with Pelicans, Puffins, Toucans and Pegasus crossings all being introduced for a variety of purposes. Not to be outdone, the Tufty Club was also introduced by the Road Safety charity RoSPA in 1953 after one of its staff members, Elsie Mills (later to be awarded an MBE) noticed an intelligent squirrel pause by the side of the road and wait for the traffic to pass before crossing the street. No-one has yet introduced the Chicken crossing, although it might help answer the big question once and for all. The latest animal to cross the road is the yellow and black striped Tiger crossing that has been tested in Aylesbury, allowing pedestrians and cyclists to safely cross together. It was not deemed a success in Buckinghamshire but has been deployed to good effect in Switzerland and Hong Kong.

Zebra crossings are now found all over the world in many English-speaking countries such as Australia, New Zealand, Canada, and the USA as well as Singapore, Holland, Germany and some Scandinavian countries.

In 1955-6 Slough was also the scene for two years of accident prevention work called somewhat dramatically 'The Slough Experiment'; it involved something currently being recreated by Sustrans under the name of 'Safe Routes to Schools'. Obviously there is nothing new under the sun, but it is shameful that well over 50 years later the same problem has still not been adequately addressed. The Slough Experiment also saw the first use of a device now installed (even if not always working) in little yellow-faced boxes on sinister grey poles... yes, you might have guessed it, the radar speedometer trap was first tried out in Slough.

An invitation to contribute your stories of the bizarre

This book is but a simple taste of the bizarre in the wacky banquet of life. The full menu is 'out there', somewhere, and I suspect that the readers of this book might know some of the missing key ingredients. It is widely understood by researchers of unusual phenomena that only a tiny proportion of strange events are ever reported either because of a fear of personal ridicule or that there is nowhere to report them to in the first place. Be reassured that those perceived problems are not ones shared here. So, this is an invitation to contribute to the database of weird and wonderful stuff of all things bizarrely Berkshire.

There is a related possibility that if enough stories are generated by readers then Two Rivers Press might be pressed, squeezed and squashed into shaping up to publish another volume of *Bizarrer Berkshire*. Any authenticated stories sent in by readers will be fully recognised if used in print. To facilitate this transfer of knowledge please email me at Duncan@tworiverspress.com or write using paper, ink, stamps, envelopes etc to Two Rivers Press, 7 Denmark Road, Reading, Berkshire, RG1 5PA or, if it will save time, just project your thoughts on the subject using mental telepathy... just kidding.

For reporting details of any unusual phenomenon it would be helpful to include: date, time, witness names, *precise* location, weather conditions, directions (if moving) and any specific aspects of size, shape and behaviour or animal reactions.

INDEX

Two Rivers Press has been publishing in and about Reading since 1994. Founded by the artist Peter Hay (1951–2003), the press continues to delight readers, local and further afield, with its varied list of individually designed, thought-provoking books.

TWO RIVERS PRESS